stretch

stretch

lessons in faith from the life of daniel

Gerard Kelly

First published 2005 by Spring Harvest Publishing Division
and Authentic Media
9 Holdom Avenue, Bletchley, Milton Keynes, Bucks, MK1 1QR, UK
and 129 Mobilization Drive, Waynesboro, GA 30830-4575, USA
www.authenticmedia.co.uk

British Library Cataloguing in Publication Data
A catalogue record for this book is available from the British Library

ISBN 1-85078-632-1

Cover design by fourninezero design.
Typeset by Temple Design
Print Management by Adare Carwin
Printed and Bound by J. H. Haynes & Co. Ltd., Sparkford

Contents

Dedication

To Chrissie, my partner and best friend of twenty-five years – with love and thanks, and in trembling anticipation of the adventure that is only just beginning…

Acknowledgements

Huge thanks are due to my family, who saw me through a very pressured writing period to bring this book to birth. Thanks also to Al Hirsch, Ben Wickham, Pete Phillips, Tim Dakin, Ajith Fernando, Viv Thomas, Pete Grieg and Andy Thornton. Though they may not know it, nor recognise their influence, they have each contributed ideas, inspiration and language to this work.

Thanks to Ernest Lucas, Mary Evans and Stephen Gaukroger, whose comments on the book of Daniel, offered in the context of the *Spring Harvest 2005 Study Guide*, have also been so helpful in the writing of this book.

Thanks to Pete Broadbent, Steve Chalke, Ian Coffey, Ruth Dearnley, Alan Johnson, Jeff Lucas and Rachael Orrell, valued fellow travellers on the journey into Daniel's world.

Thanks to Steven May-Miller, Stephanie Heald, Ali Hull and all involved in Spring Harvest Publishing, and to the wonderful Head Office team at Spring Harvest.

Thanks to all those who at different stages of my life have challenged me to stretch my faith – those I have mentioned in this text and those I haven't.

Special thanks to Dave and Amy Roche and David and Blythe Toll, who have given so much to share with us in the forging of the Bless Network.

Author Biography

Gerard Kelly is co-founder, with his wife Chrissie, of the Bless Network, a UK-based mission agency specialising in ministry to the post-Christendom cultures of mainland Europe. A popular writer and speaker, Gerard is a member of the Spring Harvest Leadership Team and author of that event's 2005 Study Guide *Sing the Lord's Song in a Strange Land*. His books have been published in the UK, the USA, France, Finland and Germany. Other titles published with Spring Harvest are *Humanifesto: A Rough Guide to the Sermon on the Mount* and *The Six Habits of Highly Connected People*. Gerard and Chrissie have four children and live in the village of Arley, on the banks of the Severn in Worcestershire.

By the rivers of Babylon we sat and wept
  when we remembered Zion.
There on the poplars
  we hung our harps,
for there our captors asked us for songs,
  our tormentors demanded songs of joy;
  they said, 'Sing us one of the songs of Zion!'
How can we sing the songs of the LORD
  while in a foreign land?

Psalm 137:1-4

introduction

Stretch, *stretch, v.t.* to extend: to draw out: to expand, make longer or wider by tension: to spread out: to reach out: to exaggerate, strain or carry further than is right: to lay at full length: to lay out: to place so as to reach from point to point or across a space... *Chambers Dictionary*[1]

Rare to be a Daniel?

Tony Benn is one of the towering figures of British politics of the twentieth century. Often unpopular for his hard-line left wing views, he is nonetheless widely respected as a passionate orator and a consummate parliamentarian. In all, he spent fifty years in the House of Commons, retiring in 2001 so that he could return to his constituency and 'spend more time in politics.' Whether as a front-line player or a back-seat observer, Benn has been involved in some of the most significant moves and moments of living memory in Westminster. His passionate opposition to the Iraq war, in the months following his retirement as an MP, gave ample evidence that his views had not mellowed with age.

So it is significant that the title he chose for his first volume of autobiography, published in 2004, did not come from contemporary politics at all but from the Bible. *Dare to be a Daniel*[2] recalls Benn's earliest years, when his mother would read to him nightly from the Bible. She always made a clear distinction, he says, between 'the Kings of Israel who exercised power and the prophets of Israel who preached righteousness.' Benn is in no doubt as to where her sympathies lay. 'I was brought up to believe in the prophets rather than the kings', he writes.

Benn's choice of title says a lot about the roots of his radicalism, which he has always attributed more to the Bible than to Marxism: but it also says something about Daniel.

It seems remarkable, in the increasingly post-Christian ethos of British politics and public life, that the phrase 'dare to be a Daniel' should still have currency – but it does. This Hebrew hero, who stood as a minority of one at the court of pagan kings and yet turned the fortunes of the empire around; this political operator who was also a person of prayer; this wise and tactful prophet who dreamed of a different future for God's people: there is something about this man.

Daniel remains one of the most influential figures in the biblical record. Generations of Jews and Christians have been empowered and inspired by his story. Yet it remains true that a 'Daniel Attitude' is all too rare in the contemporary church. The courage and power to swim against the tide of majority opinion; to recognise and resist the idols of our context and culture; to value depth over relevance: these were perhaps common features of the church of a bygone age. They are less so in ours. Maintaining belief whilst living in Babylon – singing the Lord's song in a strange land – is a deeply challenging concept.

I have come to appreciate the story of Daniel with new depth in recent months, for two reasons.

Firstly, because Daniel's context, though utterly different from ours, speaks so directly to us. The description of our current post-Christendom culture as a kind of 'exile' can be overstated, but who can fail to see in Daniel's losses the echoes of our own? Power, prestige and the visible victory of God were all lost on Daniel's journey from Jerusalem to Babylon and he could be forgiven for believing that Yahweh was finished as a viable deity. The many Christians who have begun to feel in recent years that they are singing God's song 'in a strange land' will take courage from Daniel's triumph, as he learns to worship God in an entirely foreign environment.

Secondly, because this is, above all, a chronicle of faith. The book of Daniel records the adventures of a man so in love with the worship of Yahweh that even when every support to that worship is taken from him, he holds on. Without the dimension of faith, the book makes no sense at all. And yet none of its action takes place in a temple and little of it has to do with 'religious' life. This is as much a secular as a sacred story. Daniel wrestles with his destiny in the real world. To borrow the title of Martin Robinson's and Dwight Smith's 2003 book, Daniel's whole life was a question of *Invading Secular Space*.[3] And in this, against all odds, he triumphed. I am moved as I read of Daniel's achievements because I sense that, whatever else we might need in the years ahead, we will need that kind of faith.

The suggestion that 'exile' is a reliable description of our present condition is gaining ground amongst theologians and social observers, not least through the hugely creative work of scholar Walter Brueggemann. But this does not mean that scholars are being negative about our present circumstances. There is evident pain in an exile experience and this must be acknowledged and expressed, but I want to agree with Brueggemann that exile is more an opportunity than a threat. If you were to sum up in one sentence the thesis of this book, it would be this

> The Christian community in twenty-first century Europe is in a kind of exile, and this is likely to get worse before it gets better, but it is in exile that true faith is born. It is the very losses we face that can lead, in due course, to the re-birth of authentic Christianity in Europe.

We will look for the clues to this rebirth of faith by exploring some of the best-known stories from the life of Daniel and his fellow exiles. In each, we will seek out lessons in faith to transform our own exilic journey, asking how the experiences some twenty-six centuries ago of a small band of Hebrews at the Babylonian court might offer us principles for faith in our own lives.

There will be no props to bolster his faith

The central thread that weaves these stories together over a seventy-year-long public career is that of 'faith in a foreign land'. Daniel thrives in a city in which the language and customs are alien to him; in which gods other than his own are worshipped; in which the hopes and dreams of everyday life are not those of his childhood. He learns early in life that there will be no props to bolster his faith: if it is not internally sustained, it will not last. He discovers that if he is to communicate, he must do so across a vast cultural and religious divide. The language of Jerusalem will not serve him if he is to make himself understood in Babylon. He realises that he must keep alive the dream of God's greater purposes. If he forgets, there is no one to remind him. Like an agent sent behind enemy lines, he must navigate an unfamiliar landscape.

The crucial lesson of Daniel's experience is that difficult experiences – which seem at first to stand against everything that makes faith viable – can be the very things that stretch faith to its full potential. Where others might see their faith broken by an experience of exile, as some in Babylon no doubt did, Daniel's faith becomes wider, deeper and stronger. Impossibly stretched between Jerusalem and Babylon; between the visible victory of Yahweh and his apparent defeat at the hands of foreign gods; between the power of temple and palace and the powerlessness of an unsupported faith; between the Promised Land and the prison of exile: Daniel discovers a faith that thrives in hostile soil. Like the people of Israel whose journey is somehow personified in his life, Daniel emerges with a stronger grasp of who God is, of what he is doing in the world and of the enormity of his audacious plans for humanity. On the journey from Jerusalem to Babylon, Daniel loses sight of the kingdom of Israel. But in the deprivations of exile, he finds a new vision of the kingdom of God.

One of the books that deeply influenced me as a teenager was an exploration of the workings of faith by J. B. Phillips. I don't now remember its content in great detail, but I have never forgotten its title: *Your God is Too Small*.[4] Had Phillips been alive and writing a few millennia earlier, he could have given such a book to the Hebrew exiles. This was the implicit message of the exile experience: the surprising light at the end of a very dark tunnel. Through loss came the discovery of a bigger view of God. But not all saw and knew it. Few eyes were able to see the magnificence of this light: a light that in its brightness and permanence dwarfed the very tunnel itself. When the glories of God seem to be in the past; when present experience is challenging: rare indeed is the faith that sees and celebrates the majesty of God's promised future. This is the quality of faith that grows in Daniel's life through the dark experience of exile. Far from shrinking back in the face of adversity, Daniel allows his world-view to be stretched by the mystery of God's actions. Babylon unlocks, for him, a deeper faith.

This book will explore seven characteristics of this 'stretched and stretching faith', asking whether we might have access to the same.

In **Daniel Chapter 1**, we will discover the reality of an **INTRINSIC** faith: a faith so fully internalised that it shapes everything. Had Daniel relied on the outward symbols and support structures of faith, the journey from Jerusalem to Babylon would have been fatal to that faith. But he didn't. He discovered a portable faith: a faith as deep as DNA that travelled with him no matter what the journey, bringing its influence to bear on every aspect of his life. What difference might a carry-anywhere, intrinsic faith make in our increasingly mobile, shape-shifting world?

Daniel Chapter 2 will introduce us to an **ACOUSTIC** faith: a faith grounded in the learned art of listening. Whatever other talents Daniel carried into Babylon, he carried an open ear. He engaged fully with his new environment, quickly learning its contours and complications. He was unafraid to take on a pagan education and to become proficient in a pagan tongue. His remarkable gifts of wisdom and discernment and his ability to speak God's word into the very centre of a foreign king's life were hugely magnified by the supernatural intervention of God – but they were skills built on his extraordinary capacity to listen. This exile's adventures are a compelling early picture of the art more recently called 'double-listening'.[5] With one ear tuned to the culture and the other straining for God's whisper, Daniel shows that the call of a prophet is double-edged. How might an acoustic faith, grounded in active listening, transform our relationship with the twenty-first century's diverse and changing cultures?

The focus of **Daniel Chapter 3** shifts from Daniel himself to three of his closest friends and fellow exiles, though Daniel remains a silent presence behind the scenes. In Shadrach, Meshach and Abednego we are introduced to an **ELASTIC** faith: a faith that is stretched but not broken by adversity. Facing the ultimate test of a death sentence, the faith these three young Hebrews proclaim is a double-edged sword: God *is* able to save them but even if he *doesn't*, he is still God. This is a faith that can embrace the suffering with the joy: a faith that accepts every experience God allows and from within it sings redemption's song. This is faith more steeped in tenacity than triumphalism, more geared to endurance than escape. The exiles find that it is in the fire that God meets them and adversity brings out the elasticity of their faith. Might such an elastic faith better equip us to face the tests that an increasingly hostile culture brings our way?

Daniel Chapter 4 is a narrative of power, in which the power and politics interplay in the life of a world-dominating king. Beside this great emperor, Daniel is impotent: and yet it is Daniel's God, at the last, who is worshipped. Daniel is sustained by a **KENOTIC** faith: a faith that does not seek power but thrives from a starting point of weakness and self-emptying. Kenosis is a biblical concept rooted in Philippians 2, which describes the self-emptying by which Jesus became flesh, endured death and was exalted beyond death. Daniel stands before Nebuchadnezzar, Belshazzar and Darius, just as Jesus will later stand before Pilate; and the great power of empire and might is contrasted with the inner power of a suffering servant. In our own lives, can a kenotic faith teach us to serve from a place of self-emptying and yet see our world's power structures transformed by God's grace?

In **Daniel Chapter 5** we will meet a **POETIC** faith, as Daniel interprets the messages of a God who speaks in riddles. A faith expressed with all the creativity that language allows, poetic faith embraces the mystery of God and seeks to win the world, not to wound it. It inspires those who hear it, lifting the eyes of the imagination to the horizon. In the adventure of poetic faith, Daniel learns to unlock the puzzles of God and so communicate with singular intensity. His communication is rich and intriguing, capturing the attention of his audience with its drama. Are we ready to engage with a culture starved of imagination, discovering by faith the God who is the poet in our midst?

It is in **Daniel Chapter 6** that we at last reach the show-stopper set-piece of the lions' den. Here Daniel faces his own ultimate test. His crisis is both caused and resolved by prayer and Daniel demonstrates the power of an **ECCENTRIC** faith: a faith rooted in a reality beyond the immediate. He is unafraid to be different, engaged with his culture but anchored beyond it and held by that anchor when troubles come. Daniel holds to his commitment to worshipping Yahweh, a God who seems to have no power, even at the risk of being ridiculed by those more deeply wedded to the immediate. How might the rediscovery of such a faith restore, in our time, a people who are both engaged with their culture and at that same time centred elsewhere?

The prophetic dream recorded for us in **Daniel Chapter 7** is offered as a vision of the future, painting a sky-wide canvas of the purposes of God in history. Daniel displays a **PANORAMIC** faith: a faith that sees his own small troubles against the wider vision of God's plans. Daniel is both macro-visual (seeing the big picture) and micro-active (involved in the local detail). He is dwarfed by the hugeness of God's plan for the world, and yet he knows the significance of his own obedience. Could

He is dwarfed by the hugeness of God's plan for the world

the renewal of a panoramic faith, globally connected and locally engaged, re-energise our sense of mission?

To conclude we will jump to the very end of **Daniel Chapter 12**, where we will see in the book's closing words that Daniel is urged towards a faith that finds joy in the everyday realities of being human. Daniel is sent back into exile – back into ordinary experience – to live out his workaday calling in the stretching realities of the routine. He has experienced the heights of prophetic adventure but his ultimate calling is to the ordinary. Whatever else faith is to mean for Daniel, it is to mean an ordinary human life transformed by God's evident presence. How might our culture be impacted today by a faith that honours humanity and elevates the ordinary?

These seven characteristics of Daniel's stretched and stretching faith are revealed in the different circumstances he and his Hebrew colleagues face in Babylon. My sense is that they represent seven areas in which we would do well to ask God to stretch our faith, in our very different settings. They are seven 'keys' that can together create a faith that will thrive in exile: that will not be snuffed out by the harsh winds of opposition but made stronger through them.

Working with churches in the UK and on mainland Europe as well as in Australia and the United States, and speaking with emerging young leaders in all these settings, I have a growing sense of the significance of 'faith' as an aspect of the Christian journey for our time. In the circles I move in, which would broadly be described as mainstream charismatic and evangelical, we talk widely about what the church ought to look like to be accessible to those around us. We have discussed cultural relevance at great length and have invested millions in making worship contemporary and sermons 'seeker' friendly. This is not hyperbole: the churches of the west have quite literally invested millions in these areas in recent years. It might even be billions. We have abandoned, to a greater or lesser degree, some of our dogmatic opinions and adversarial style. We have sought to address many of our cultural and historical blind spots. We are learning to listen to our peers outside the church. All this is good and helpful but if I have a fear, it is that this might mean that we have invested less time in *building faith*. We pour a great deal more, it seems, into making sure that the saints are comfortable with their Christian experience than into equipping those same saints for the works of service God may have for them. Why is it that even with the growth and splendour of our churches, it is so rare to find believers who as individuals are strong, confident, established and effective in their faith? In many places, I believe, we have forgotten what it takes to build people of faith.

Much as I love being in the many churches that I have the privilege to visit, I do find myself struck – sometimes at the most inappropriate moments, when the worship is as good as it gets and excellence is all around like snowfall – by one of the strangest questions Jesus ever asked: 'When the Son of Man comes, will he find faith on the earth?'[6]

Faith is, according to Hebrews 11:1, 'being sure of what we hope for, and certain of what we do not see.' Faith is the capacity to go on believing when the external supports are taken away. It is an inner strength; an inner grip on a reality so powerful, so all-withstanding that even the most devastating change in outer conditions does not change it. People of faith are deep people – they are people who make more of a dent on their circumstances than their circumstances make on them. This is the brand of faith that 'the ancients were commended for'[7] but is it a brand of faith that is less and less evident in the churches of the west? And might it offer us the very vitamins we need to withstand the viruses ahead?

On a frosty day toward the end of December 2004, I received an e-mail from a man I am proud to call a friend, who has served as a model of faith for me for over ten years. His name is Ajith Fernando, and he is the leader of Youth for Christ's ministry in Sri Lanka. His e-mail was written just three days after the world's largest earthquake in recent memory had turned the ocean around Sri Lanka into a raging monster and swept away thousands in a few terrible minutes of utter devastation. Ajith had been forced to cancel a writing sabbatical for which he had been preparing for months and to join with others in helping where he could in the relief efforts. His e-mail did not revel in garish descriptions of the tsunami's aftermath. Rather it asked for prayer for the workers who had thrown themselves into the urgent tasks of rescue and repair; for their strength and well-being; for their lives of prayer and devotion; for their integrity and inner health. Ajith's deepest longing was that in the midst of such heart-wrenching suffering, his team would find the time they needed to pray and to seek God and that Scripture would be to them a source of strength and solace. What is faith worth if it cannot feed us when all seems lost?

Whenever I think of people of faith in the world today, Ajith comes to mind. A Bible teacher respected internationally for his skills as a speaker and writer, he has more than once turned down significant conference invitations to be free to spend time with the young people served through YFC's programmes in Sri Lanka. In a nation

wracked by civil war over many years, he has seen his best
workers intimidated and harassed; he has seen talented
Christians leaving the country in great numbers as
opportunities abroad offer
security and peace; he has
wrestled with the call to work
amongst the poor when it
would be so easy not to. All
who meet him are moved by his faith and integrity. The
terrible impact of the Christmas tsunami on Sri Lanka is
the latest chapter in a catalogue of distress and yet Ajith
and those like him are driven not by despair but by faith.
Though much is lost and worse still may be threatened,
theirs is a faith that can withstand.

**Theirs is a faith
that can withstand**

Speaking of his own faith journey, Ajith resists any
tendency by others to see him as a hero. 'I am a struggling
Christian,' he says.

> Perhaps I have done OK in some areas but I have done
> badly in areas that may not be visible to others. My wife
> knows. We each face challenges as Christians. My biggest
> struggles have not been with materialism and safety etc.
> They are minor in comparison to the struggle to keep my
> mind pure, especially when I travel; and also to be decisive,
> with a strong moral cutting edge. My indecisiveness is a
> source of consternation to my colleagues. This is why I do
> not think I am in anyway special. I have survived in some
> areas and continue to struggle in others.

But for all this, from where I stand Ajith has been an
inspiration and a model. I see a faith at work in his life that
I covet for my own: a faith that has the courage to seek
God's way of integrity and service even when an easier
route seems open. On the days when I have been tempted

to take the soft road; when obedience has seemed so hard, the glimpses I have seen of Ajith's life and faith have restored my focus. I covet such conviction. I aspire to such faith. And I have to admit to its rarity – in my own life and in the lives of those whose Christian journey seems closest to mine.

This is a book about building faith; about taking the seeds of faith we do have and asking God to grow them. It is about being stretched beyond the norm, beyond our half-hearted expectations. Inspired and informed by Daniel's 'exile diaries', it holds out the hope that such a faith is possible in our confusing times and that those who embrace it might find themselves witnessing a rebirth of Christianity in a post-Christian age.

The ultimate triumph of Daniel is that he does better in Babylon than many of his fellow-Jews had done in Jerusalem. The absence of the symbols and support mechanisms of religion does not rob him of his faith, it makes him stronger. Exile serves to purify, deepen and strengthen his faith. It causes him to think harder, pray **Exile serves to purify** longer and look deeper. The result is a series of prophecies that in many ways lay the foundations for the ministry of Jesus and the discovery that God has a much bigger plan than to bless Israel alone. Through the losses of deportation and dislocation, Daniel gains a deep, abiding and exhilarating faith. Exile is good for him.

Do we need to ask ourselves, just as the exile generation of Jerusalem were forced to, whether we have become too dependent on the external props and provisions of a 'Christendom' faith? Are we so used to worshipping in large crowds that we have forgotten how to be alone? Are we so in need of public sympathy for our faith that we have forgotten how to face hostility and conflict? Are we so attracted to power that we can no longer embrace a ministry of weakness? Have we become so comfortable with our wealth that the fear of poverty – the normal experience for huge numbers of Christians across the planet – enslaves us? Exile meant for Daniel a loss of power and prestige. It involved relocation to a foreign culture and the learning of a new language. It meant facing hostility and explaining faith in Yahweh to people entirely outside that experience. And yet it became, for him, not a curse but a blessing. It brought him into a life that he would never have enjoyed if the city of God had not fallen.

What faith adventures await us, beyond the walls of Christendom, out there in the 'foreign soil' of a changed and changing culture? What depths of faith and wisdom might God have for us to discover? What dreams might he yet have to give us? My reading of the book of Daniel suggests that the blessings cannot be ours without the letting go – that renewal lies somewhere beyond relinquishment. There is an adventure of faith waiting for us in the twenty-first century. There are new languages to learn, new cultures to explore; whole new Babylons to be invaded by eccentric prophets. It's cold out there but it's in the cold places that the muscles of faith prosper most. Are you ready to leave Jerusalem behind?

s t r e t c hing exercises

As you prepare for a journey of exploration of Daniel's stretched and stretching faith, here are three questions to consider:

Daniel

The introduction suggests that Daniel is a key figure in our religious consciousness, even among those who have little or no active faith. Has this been true in your experience? What images does the phrase 'dare to be a Daniel' conjure up for you? Are they inviting or off-putting? If the journey we are about to undertake is rooted in the life of Daniel, what are you most looking forward to discovering, or doing as a result?

Take a moment to pray. Thank God for the life of this man Daniel, whose legacy has so shaped the church. Thank God for this book of Daniel, the words of which have inspired believers in every generation. Ask God if there are goals you should set for yourself on this journey. Let him know that you are open to thinking new thoughts; to hearing new words; to growing and developing in your faith. Let the prayer 'Father, stretch my faith' become your watchword as you read.

Faith

Is faith an area in which you feel strong or weak? Is it something you long for more of? What kinds of things might you do in your life if your faith began to grow? What do you dream of achieving?

Take time to pray for the deepening and nurturing of your faith. On a scale of 1 to 10, ask God to help you assess where your faith is now and where you might like it to be. Ask God, even now, to begin to show you ways in which you can strengthen your faith.

Stretching

Take a few moments – standing or lying down, whichever you prefer – to stretch your body. Start with your feet and ankles then, working up through your legs, thighs, diaphragm, chest, arms and neck, stretch each muscle you can. After each stretch, relax.

Now pray quietly: 'Creator God, as I have stretched each muscle of my body, may I stretch just as boldly the muscles of my faith. May I grow stronger in your knowledge, wiser in your wisdom and deeper in your love. In Jesus' name. Amen.'

CHAPTER ONE

intrinsic

In the third year of the reign of Jehoiakim king of Judah, Nebuchadnezzar king of Babylon came to Jerusalem and besieged it. And the LORD delivered Jehoiakim king of Judah into his hand, along with some of the articles from the temple of God. These he carried off to the temple of his god in Babylonia and put in the treasure house of his god. (Dan. 1:1,2)

intrinsic, –al, *adjs.*, inward: genuine: inherent: essential, belonging to the point at issue: (of muscles) entirely contained within the limb and girdle. *Chambers Dictionary*[8]

intrinsic faith: faith so deeply rooted, it shapes everything

burning books

When Michael Moore made his controversial film *Fahrenheit 9/11*, which won the Palme D'Or at the 2004 Cannes Film Festival, he was not only ridiculing the American administration. He was also paying an oblique tribute to a film made almost forty years earlier. The 1966 science-fiction adventure *Fahrenheit 451* was, in its day, as innovative as Moore's later documentary. Based on Ray Bradbury's book,[9] which now has five million copies in print, the film was directed by French new-wave icon Francois Truffaut. Its title is a reference to the temperature at which books will burn – the combustion point of paper. In Bradbury's futuristic world, a totalitarian government has banned books, assuming them to be a subversive influence on all who read them. Firemen, including the film's hero Montag, are not those who extinguish fires but those who start them, employed by the government to seek out and burn all books, along with the homes they are found in. The aim of this policy is simple and clearly stated: to rid the world of every book ever written.

The film's most moving segment is its ending, acknowledged by many as a classic sequence of 1960s cinema. Crossing over to the resistance movement, Montag is eventually taken to a secret camp in the woods, where pro-book activists have found an innovative means of defying the government's plans. Their fear is that even if they collect and hide books, these will eventually be found and destroyed. But memories cannot be erased so easily. Holding on to single copies of the classics of literature, each person volunteers not only to read the book, but to *become* it, learning the text by heart in order to preserve and pass it on. In an ironic reference to the originator of the idea, one character in the film introduces himself to Montag as 'Martian Chronicles. I am *The Martian Chronicles* by Ray Bradbury.' Trying to save books from the fire is not enough, such is the reach and determination of the government's anti-book hit squads. But memories cannot be burned at any temperature, as long as those carrying them have breath. *Books* will be kept alive by the people who internalise them; carrying them, by definition, wherever they go.

> **Volunteers not only to read the book, but to *become* it**

I want to suggest that this evocative image, of people so committed to books that they will *become* them, is a valuable metaphor of the faith that Daniel and his friends needed in Babylon – and that we need today. This is not a faith entirely dependent on crowds, meetings, drum-kits and rousing preachers. Nor is it a faith that will crumble as soon as our props are taken away. It is a faith, rather, that has been internalised; a faith through which God's story becomes so much a part of us that we *become* God's story. It is an intrinsic faith, woven into the very codes of our existence; buried so deep in our DNA that no external force can snuff it out.

Daniel is stretched by the experience of exile because he is taken away from every external support that he might have leaned on to bolster his faith. A measurable, physical distance is created between him and the sources of his strength. *He is stretched across the vast gap between the roots and rhythms of the faith he has grown up with and the hard cold place in which he is called to express it.* But there is a resilience in Daniel that his Babylonian captors have not anticipated. As he is dragged far from Jerusalem, he does not lose his faith *because his faith travels with him.* It is portable, internalised – a 'faith to go.' Whatever else has happened to Daniel in his youth, something has enabled him to so 'ingest' faith in Yahweh that it is with him wherever he goes.

into exile

Chapter 1 of the book of Daniel is a scene-setter, leaving us in no doubt that there are few supports left in place to encourage Daniel and his friends to keep their faith. They are taken to Babylon as part of a group drawn from the higher echelons of Jewish society. These young men are to be re-educated and trained for service in the Babylonian empire. The programme for their assimilation is to begin immediately. The chapter sees our heroes making the journey from Jerusalem to Babylon and settling in to their new situation. It describes in detail three key aspects of this exile experience

These young men are to be re-educated and trained for service

- the extensive programme of education and orientation that these young men were to receive – preparing them for top level jobs in the Babylonian civil service.
- the decision by the official in charge of this programme to rename its participants, giving them names derived from the worship of Babylonian gods.
- the 'act of resistance' organised by Daniel and undertaken by all four of the group, whereby they choose to fast from

the high-quality food brought from the palace kitchen, and live instead on vegetables and water. The success of this diet forms the dramatic climax of this first chapter.

A number of facts are woven into this narrative that set the tone for all that will follow in the story of Daniel.

The context: exile. We are told that the unfolding story will take place in the context of a forced removal from Jerusalem to Babylon. Though Daniel and his friends are well housed, well fed and well treated, they are effectively imprisoned. Far from home, they have lost the power and privilege associated with their prominent families in Jerusalem. Though Daniel is not included by many scholars among the prophets of exile, this is nonetheless an exile narrative, built on the dislocation and loss of the journey from Jerusalem to Babylon.

The issue: faith. The taking of sacred articles from the Jerusalem temple indicates that this is a spiritual as well as a political victory. There is a conflict between Babylon and Israel, in which Israel is the loser. But behind this there is an implied conflict between the gods of Babylon and Israel's God, Yahweh. One of the primary questions that the book of Daniel will wrestle with is this: 'Is it Israel that has lost power, or *the God of Israel?*' On the surface, we wonder if Daniel can survive the experience of exile but far more deeply the book is asking us if Yahweh can survive it. Is God's 'turf' limited to the Promised Land – or will he still be God when all is lost?

The threat: assimilation. It is clear from the text that Nebuchadnezzar has initiated a programme of *assimilation* rather than *oppression*. His aim is to win Daniel and his friends over to the superiority and wisdom of the

Babylonian world-view and through them to influence other Jews. The decision to bring prominent members of a conquered culture into key roles in the service of the conquering empire is an established strategy of assimilation, by which the empire gets the best out of each new territory it invades. Later in the book this benevolent assimilation will become harsh oppression and the possibility of violence is never far below the surface, but in its wider context the narrative deals as much with *seduction* as with *suffering*.

The hero: Daniel. At the beginning of Chapter 1, Daniel is one name amongst four: by the end of the chapter he is clearly the leader of the group. We aren't told whether this status was already in place in Jerusalem, but once in Babylon Daniel demonstrates the initiative, courage and faith that set him apart. The wisdom with which he *accepts* a new name but *rejects* the king's food marks him out as a leader of remarkable perception and creativity. We are presented, in the person of Daniel, with a model response to conditions of exile.

The chapter sets up the dramatic tension which will drive forward the unfolding of Daniel's story. What will become of this young man, who has dared to resist the will of the emperor and to question the power of the empire's gods? Will the empire crush him, or will he survive? Whose God, in the long term, will prove strongest? Will Daniel find the inner resources – the strength, courage and hope – to thrive in the face of such an onslaught of assimilation? He has been taken to the very belly of the beast, the dark heart of a world-dominating empire. This is no satellite space-station: it is the Death Star itself. Far from the sound of the Psalms and the gentle glow

Can Daniel keep his faith?

of the temple lamps; far from the golden stones of Jerusalem and the olive groves of Israel; far from the myths and memories that have made Hebrew history: can Daniel keep his faith?

they think it's all over...

The central character of this drama is Daniel – but the story is about Israel. The hope of all Israel, the future of all Israel, is somehow carried in the life of this one man as he lives through – and survives – the fate all Israel has feared. Will exile destroy Israel? Will the promises of God be forgotten and the nation destroyed? Will the very memory of God's victory be lost as the saga that began with the faith of Abraham, the adventuring of Joseph and the liberating passion of Moses descends into tragedy and loss? Will the exile be the undoing of the Exodus, leaving the Hebrews in as bitter a slavery as they began with? These questions hang in the air as we watch the story unfold. How will this new experience – exile; loss; the defiling of God's temple; the 'defeat' of God himself – impact faith? Is there a plan and purpose to God's rule that can survive such a blow? Can faith stay strong in the furnace of affliction? Is there a divine courage for those who face the lions of a hostile culture?

Daniel becomes the focus of all these questions. In his faith, we see the faith of Israel projected. His sufferings are the sufferings of Israel. If he can find hope, there is hope to be found for all of us. If he can stay true to Yahweh in the face of Yahweh's defeat, perhaps we all can. The book of Daniel is more than a collection of stories aimed at encouraging struggling souls. It is more than a morality tale to uplift our hearts. It is an epic adventure; a myth on the scale of the Norse sagas, of *Moby Dick*, of *Gangs of New*

York. Other tales can serve to encourage those facing difficult times and the loss of prosperity – Daniel serves those facing the loss of God. In this book God himself – represented in the victory over Egypt, the settling of the land; the building of the temple; the sanctity of the holy city of Jerusalem; the royal Davidic line – seems lost to us. It is not we who have lost a battle, but God. Or so it seems.

Exile is a kind of death, in which not only Israel but Yahweh himself seems implicated. The God who has promised to stand against evil; who proclaims himself greater than the pagan gods; who will not allow the slavery in Egypt to continue; who rages against the pagans even as he clears them from the land: this God of victory, might and power gives in, it seems, to a pagan army. He lets a pagan king defile the Promised Land, the holy city and the sacred temple. He allows pagan worshippers to walk all over him. Where is he? Is he powerless after all? Was Moses wrong about him?

It is difficult to over-estimate the significance of the exile to the Hebrew people. Their whole relationship with their God, Yahweh, was based on a covenant or agreement. They would worship and obey him and he, in return, would bless them. This special relationship would be made visible in three key ways: the Hebrew people would have a land of their own with God's city, Jerusalem, at its heart; they would have descendants to safeguard their nation into the future and they would enjoy the continued, visible protection of God for his people. He would fight for them. He would rescue them, just as he did at the Red Sea. He would be their Deliverer. Imagine, then, their shock and distress when they are taken once more into slavery. Exile was, for the Hebrew people, a corporately experienced car crash: a national invitation to post-traumatic stress disorder.

He would fight for them

is daniel's story our story?

The experience of the exiles is relevant to us today because our situation parallels theirs in so many ways. Like them, it would be all too easy for us to look back with rose-tinted spectacles and see a 'Christian' past that never really existed but like them, we must take account of the very real losses we have suffered in recent years. Stuart Murray, in his comprehensive study *Post-Christendom*,[10] has summarised the seven key transitions which together mark out the parameters of our journey from a Christendom to a post-Christendom context. This 'journey into exile' will take the church

From the centre to the margins: in Christendom the Christian story and the churches were central, but in post-Christendom they are marginal.

From majority to minority: in Christendom Christians comprised the (often overwhelming) majority, but in post-Christendom we are a minority.

From settlers to sojourners: in Christendom Christians felt at home in a culture shaped by their story, but in post-Christendom we are aliens, exiles and pilgrims in a culture in which we no longer feel at home.

From privilege to plurality: in Christendom Christians enjoyed many privileges, but in post-Christendom we are one community among many in a plural society.

From control to witness: in Christendom churches could exert control over society, but in post-Christendom we exercise influence only through our witnessing to our story and its implications.

From maintenance to mission: in Christendom the emphasis was on maintaining a supposedly Christian status quo, but in post-Christendom it is on mission within a contested environment.

From institution to movement: in Christendom churches operated mainly in institutional mode, but in post-Christendom we must become again a Christian movement.

These seven transitions add up to a 'life-change' for the Christian church in western culture; a corporate loss of power, prestige and privilege. They will take us to a place that is difficult to deal with and get used to, but in which there is much to learn. Like evacuees coming to a new environment, our names tied to us on parcel labels in case we forget them, we will have to *exercise* our faith in surroundings that are significantly different from those in which we have *developed* our faith.

It is important here to note that we are describing the feelings associated with exile, rather than the experience of exile itself. Our situation is not the same as that faced by Daniel; just as Daniel's own exile was not in every way the same as the exile of all Israel. There are historical, theological and circumstantial factors surrounding the deportation of the Jews to Babylon that are simply not present in our own lives. But the metaphor of exile has gained new currency in recent years because the journey from a Christendom to a post-Christendom have the character of a kind of exile. Some of the power and privilege that were once associated with the Christian church in our society has been lost. There is a sense in which the faith once so central to our culture is

When changes like this occur, it can *feel* a lot like exile

increasingly being pushed to its margins. When changes like this occur, it can *feel* a lot like exile.

The greater truth is that this sense of exile may be the road to our liberation. What seems at first a terrible loss may prove to be a great gain. Just as Daniel discovered, in exile, the broad horizons of God's greater purposes, so we might find that what we thought was our exile turns out, in the end, to be our Exodus.

We are not, as the church, in a punished exile from God: we are called on a positive mission that leads us to live as pilgrims in this world, bearing witness to a different reality. If we have a home and a destination, then we are not wandering aimlessly. If we are entrusted with the foretaste of freedom in order to tell others of it then we are on this mission not as victims, but as empowered 'sent ones' and our post-Christendom situation is not to be lamented but celebrated. Perhaps the binding together of church and state in the histories of Europe has been our captivity – perhaps its end is our freedom. We can now really be the church in Europe, rather than a puppet of the establishment. Perhaps this is our destiny, our release: a kind of exile that turns out to be the door to hope.[11]

When I was ten years old my parents separated and I moved with my mother from Canada to England. For five years I had been shaped for survival in the Canadian playground. I had learned to skate and to play ice hockey. I knew the names of the leading players. I was no great hockey player but I could hold my own. Then, in an instant, my world changed. In my new playground teams were chosen for football, not hockey. I didn't know my Hotspurs from my Uniteds: I didn't even know where Manchester was. I had never learned to kick a ball. I had none of the skills needed for this strange environment and I soon got used to being picked last or not at all. Overnight I moved from the centre to the margins; from the heart of the party to its hesitant edge. I tasted, in my own small way, the flavour of exile.

But I learned from this experience. I began to have sympathy for the misfits who never got picked. This was not my natural leaning. I came from a family that revelled in intellectual superiority; that felt it had a right to a place at the top

I had never learned to kick a ball

table. I was at the head of the class in many subjects, and near the top in all. I had travelled widely, and enjoyed a lifestyle of relative privilege. There was nothing in my nature that would make me open my heart to those less privileged. But exile broke my superior air. Later, God took me to a Bible college where my fellow students were not my 'type'; where I had to live in a close community of people from all kinds of backgrounds. Some of them really didn't like me and I don't blame them. But I learned, step by step, to set aside my inherited and utterly false sense of superiority, and to find the image and presence of God in all kinds of people I would otherwise hold in contempt. I learned that the really fruitful place to be is often not at the centre but at the margins; that while the press and public are focused on the winners' enclosure, there are all sorts of interesting things happening elsewhere; that the weak and the dispossessed have rich lessons to teach us all. The most important lessons of my life have been learned through deprivation. Exile has been my most eloquent instructor.

Whatever flavour our faith takes on in the near future, it will be in some sense a 'faith in exile', and we have much to learn from those who have walked such roads before us. The starting point for this journey is an internalisation of faith, in terms of two key areas: *mood* and *memory*.

faith in exile as a change of mood

It is significant for Daniel that exile does not produce a change in just one aspect of his faith, nor in the ingredients of faith: it is more like a mood-shift, an atmospheric change in the whole basis of faith. He is no longer starting from the triumph of Jerusalem but from the defeat of exile. The strength that he must find is an *inner* strength. A metaphor that I have found helpful in grasping this kind of change is that of a key change in music. This is the idea captured by the great twentieth century songwriter Cole Porter, in his memorable song, *Every Time We Say Goodbye,* in which the idea of a shift from a major to a minor key serves as a metaphor for the sense of loss that comes with the breaking of a relationship.

How strange the change: from majority to minority; from dominance to diminution; from the mainstream to the margins. This metaphor seems to me to resonate with the current journey of the church because this is a *strange change* we are confronting. These are not logical changes, each specifically dictated by

You can't draw little arrows on a map to show what's happening

clearly identifiable social forces. You can't draw little arrows on a map to show what's happening. These are deep changes in the soul of western culture. They are a mood shift, often expressed in attitudes that are strongly felt but hard to explain; frustrations that overwhelm but defy articulation. The idea of a key change powerfully captures our situation, because a key change affects everything about a piece of music – not only which notes are played and how they connect together, but also the total 'feel' of the piece. This is the very strangeness that many Christians are feeling in this time of transition. It is not that one or two things have completely changed – it is that *everything* has in some way changed.

faith in C-minor

The major keys are used to sing of triumph, of celebration. Military marches are written in a major key, as are fanfares, wedding anthems and many of our hymns. The minor keys are reserved for lament and melancholy. They pose more questions than answers, they move forward tentatively. They ask permission to be heard. But very often, beneath this, they sing of hope. The inner certainties that lend strength to an intrinsic faith are more deeply held, somehow, than the hollow proclamations of triumphalism. They find strength in depth.

The minor keys are not by definition melancholic. It is often assumed that they are, but there can be a seriousness that does not, in itself, cause a loss of hope. One of the most passionate compositions of all time, Rachmaninov's Second Piano Concerto in C-Minor, is a stunning example of this mood.

Rachmaninov saw his First Symphony performed in 1897, to a disastrous response. The performance was poor and the conductor drunk, and the critics hated the piece. The young composer all but lost the will to create. For three years he faced an acute form of 'composer's block'. He couldn't write a note and his self-confidence as a musician dwindled. He was lost, going from one friend and advisor to another, desperate to find once again his creative energy, his power with music. In the end it was a strange mixture of mainstream and alternative therapy with the pioneering neurologist Nikolai Dahl that helped the young musician. He began daily sessions with Doctor Dahl in January of

1900 and slowly began to write again. Within four months
he was re-emerging as a composer of presence and skill.
The result was his Second Piano Concerto in C-Minor,
written in the same year. This profound composition has
been used often in films and theatre and its intense,
brooding opening chords are recognisable to millions. Its
mood of passion and melancholy provided the emotional
background to the classic love story of *Brief Encounter*, in
which tragedy and hope, passion and pain were so
delicately interlaced.

Buried deep in the romantic melancholy of
Rachmaninov's work, there is a passion for the future that
is life-enhancing, not soul destroying. This most Russian
of composers understands that it is in the deep places that
truth is to be found, even if it is also in the deep places
that loss is felt. In the lament there is a hint of elation –
not of the empty triumphalism that ignores adversity, but
of human character chiselled by pressure: character that
faces loss and yet lives. The symphony marked the
resurrection of Rachmaninov's creativity – and it carries a
resurrection tone, recognising that joy as well as sadness
can have depth. God's joys are not found in the superficial
but in weighty places, where pains as well as pleasures
are acknowledged.

Is this the kind of music God requires of us, as we 'sing
the Lord's song in a strange land'? Is he asking that we
learn to be a 'Church in C-Minor', acknowledging loss
beyond our loudness; facing questions as well as answers;
finding hope in the 'deep places' of lament? It is not only
churches that are facing decline in Europe; institutions of all
types are failing and more will follow. It is the culture itself
that is reeling. The loss, the alienation that many feel in the
church today is just a foretaste of the loss and alienation
that will ultimately grip the wider culture. 'Where there is

no revelation, the people cast off restraint; but blessed is
he who keeps the law.'[12] Might it not be, in such a time, that
a faith expressed in a minor key is the very faith that will
strike a chord among an exiled people?

If this is the case, it will affect everything about the way
we embrace and express our faith. It will give a different
flavour to our worship and prayer and to our evangelism. It
will change the way we are perceived in the wider culture,
and the basis on which we are accepted or rejected. It will
alter our expectations of God and our understanding of
God's expectations of us. We will do more whispering than
shouting, more caring for our
neighbours than cornering them. We
will create more silence than
sideshows and perhaps speak more
of *depth* than of *success*. We might
well, like Daniel, begin to
communicate with more 'wisdom
and tact'[13] than we formerly felt was
needed. We will draw in, rather than
demonise, the curious sceptic who
comes to us unable to believe. We
will be subtle and sensitive, reflective
and redemptive; cultured and curious. We will ignite the
minds of those drawn to us in order that we might enflame
their hearts; we will seek healing in our humanity so that
humans just like us might, too, be healed.

We will be subtle and sensitive, reflective and redemptive; cultured and curious

Geoff and Sandra Ryan are Salvation Army officers who
served for a number of years in Russia and Chechnya and
are now based once more in their home town of Toronto in
Canada. They work in one of the poorest areas of the city,
leading a congregation whose members come from the
wrong side of the tracks and are often on the wrong side of
the law. Geoff describes one of the most significant

moments of his life, which involved giving a cup of hot chocolate to a man sleeping rough under one of the city's many flyovers. It was part of a regular Friday night routine and Geoff had seen the man before: but there was a particular moment, on a particular night, when he came to understand that the very essence of his faith was carried, somehow, in that simple act of handing over a hot drink. It was such a small act, amongst people whose significance society had already discounted and yet to be present there, to bring a single hot drink to a man who would otherwise receive nothing, to be the bearer of a small gift whose absence would symbolise the final desolation: this was the very meaning of faith. Faith in a minor key understands that the most significant songs are not always the loudest; that the ways of God are revealed amongst the bruised and the fragile, the broken and frail. One whisper of such faith can scream louder, in the real world, than a whole brass band of empty triumph. Was this the faith that was promised in the Messiah when Isaiah said of him 'A bruised reed he will not break, and a smouldering wick he will not snuff out'?[14] Was this not the faith that was so evident in the gentle, loving life of Jesus?[15]

Jesus suggested to us that even a cup of cold water given in his name would make a difference.[16] Why not a cup of hot chocolate? Might the loss of the power and prestige so often associated with the church in the past enable us to rediscover a faith expressed in simple acts of kindness, a faith lived out amongst the powerless? A key signature change affects the feel of your performance. It calls you to a different way of being in relation to your music and your audience. Like all musical notation, it tells you what to play but it has a special, much deeper role: it tells you how to play it.

faith in exile as the guarding of memory

The second area in which Daniel's journey, and ours, calls for an internalisation of faith is in the important area of *memory*. Scholars take a range of views about the exact role of the years in Babylon in the construction of the Old Testament Scriptures, but all are agreed that this was a significant and fruitful period. With the holy land, city, temple and palace lost, it becomes more important than ever to keep alive the memory of God's story. The exiles must learn in fresh ways to indwell their story and to pass it on to their children, raised in the strange circumstances of exile. It is perhaps for this reason that Daniel chooses food – so central to the Hebrew understanding of faith – as the battleground on which he will take his disciplined stand. He is helping his friends to remember the basis on which they have loved and worshipped Yahweh. The years in Babylon become years of remembering: telling and re-telling the stories of God. As John Holdsworth notes

> **It is perhaps for this reason that Daniel chooses food**

What we see is that the great trauma of the Exile, potentially disastrous for the faith, identity and even existence of Israel, actually becomes one of the most creative periods in its theology with lots of new works being written and older traditions collected. It is because of this that we have an Old Testament at all.[17]

eat the story

In our own time and context, the equivalent process is associated with the internalising of God's word, so that Scripture becomes part of our DNA, deeply buried in the very cell structure of our being. Mike Riddell speaks of the Bible as

> ... the repository of stories ... from generations of people who have tried to follow God. It is also the bearer of 'the story of all stories': the life and teaching of Jesus ...the Bible keeps alive for us 'the dangerous memory of Jesus.'[18]

Old Testament scholar Craig Bartholomew draws attention, in this context, to the significance of God's instructions to the prophet Ezekiel at an early stage of his prophetic ministry

> Then I looked, and I saw a hand stretched out to me. In it was a scroll, which he unrolled before me. On both sides of it were written words of lament and mourning and woe.

> And he said to me, 'Son of man, eat what is before you, eat this scroll; then go and speak to the house of Israel.' So I opened my mouth, and he gave me the scroll to eat.[19]

Just as Ezekiel was challenged to eat the scroll given to him, and only then to speak God's word to Israel, so it is as the prophet 'ingests' God's written word that they are able to speak out God's spoken word. It is as we are exposed to the ways in which God has spoken in the past, carried for us in Scripture, that we are inspired and empowered to hear God's word for our own day. The believer who longs to speak, on God's behalf, a dynamic, immediate word to a given context, will be enabled to do so to the extent that they are immersed in God's written word.[20]

One of the people whose faith has most deeply stirred me in recent years is a young man named Alexander Flek (Sasha) who lives in Prague in the Czech Republic. I was introduced to Sasha by a mutual friend and immediately liked him. Converted at the age of nineteen when Czechoslovakia was still a communist state, he soon became active in evangelism and church leadership, seeing many hundreds of people come to faith. He once casually said to me in conversation, 'Being arrested was always difficult when you were on your own, but when a group were arrested together, it wasn't so bad.' I asked him in some surprise how many times he was arrested in those years.'Oh, about forty or fifty times,' he said.

When the Velvet Revolution took the Czech people out of the shadow of communism, Sasha continued to work with young adults across the city of Prague, building strong relationships with the artists, writers and other creative people who give the city its unique imaginative energy. But he was always deeply saddened by one great lack in Czech culture: there was no Bible translation in clear, contemporary Czech. The two translations available were a very early Reformed work, more archaic than the UK's Authorised Version, and a 1970s version supported by the communist regime and offering a very liberal, miracle-free narrative. Sasha longed for a simple, accessible translation that would capture the raw power and beauty of Scripture but make it available to modern and post-modern Czech people. So he set out, with a group of friends, to create one.

When I met Sasha in 1999, the work had already taken five years and had at least another five to run. Funding was intermittent and resources few. The work was demanding and detailed, and required hours of painstaking research. But he was determined to continue and see the project through to its end. The New Testament is complete and widely used. The Old Testament is on its way.

And Sasha and his friends will press on with this work until it is done; despite the many opportunities to do something more casual, less difficult and, in all likelihood, more immediately rewarding. Their faith is not rooted in the passing fashions of the day, but in the unchanging power of God's story to move and mould the hearts of men and women. Their legacy will almost certainly outlive them for generations.

> **Their faith is not rooted in the passing fashions of the day**

bible allsorts

My own journey with God has been deeply affected in recent years by following a one year Bible-reading plan. Essentially a pocket Bible with dated pages, this enables me to read each day an Old Testament section, a New Testament section, a psalm and a few verses from Proverbs. Building this habit into my daily (or perhaps every-other-daily) routine has given me a wider and deeper view of Scripture. Wider, because I am exposed to passages I dislike and struggle to understand as much as to those I know and love. Like a traveller following a trusted guide, I sometimes come across a familiar path but at other times I walk in uncharted terrain. I have found that learning comes as much from the struggles as the ease, and it is by the whole witness of Scripture that my life is shaped: by eating all the allsorts, not picking out my favourite flavours. I have gained a deeper view of Scripture because I cannot simply skate over the passages in which my 'favourite' verses are set. I cannot extract two or three 'classic texts' from Jeremiah and shelve the rest. I have to live with Jeremiah for days on end. I have to come to terms with his uncomfortable, anti-establishment, unyielding stance; with his refusal to allow the status quo to go unchallenged. I cannot drop in on Job at the beginning and end of his trials, making trite comparisons between the two – I have to walk with him through the pain and doubt; to sit by him as he wrestles with circumstances beyond enduring. I cannot read Psalm 137, with its evocative image of poplars hung with redundant harps, and ignore its later stark cry for a violent revenge. In each of these examples, I must spend time with the characters and complexities of each book, letting its depths seep into my awareness. I must allow my life to be shaped by Scripture, not seek to shape Scripture to fit my life.

I have found this an exhilarating and transforming journey: so much so that I regret the years of channel-hopping and cherry-picking, the frequent returns to the same tried and tested passages. It is part, I believe, of the internalisation of faith: part of the process by which, at a level deeper than conscious thought, I am allowing my world-view to be shaped by Scripture's witness. It gives me courage to stand firm when the idolatrous voices of my culture – massed, insistent and loud – demand my worship. It enables me, slowly but surely, to bring into obedience the areas of my life in which my reactions and responses are less godly, less holy, less redemptively human, than they should be. Many such areas remain to be conquered, and as I allow the searchlight of this internalised, God-breathed wisdom to sweep over the

Many such areas remain to be conquered

landscape of my soul, I find more such corners of resistance identified each day.

I have had cause to wonder in recent months if we are not in danger, as a contemporary church, of losing this radical exposure to Scripture. Many of us have denounced and rejected, perhaps rightly, the overly-religious practices of our forebears. Tony Benn has not continued his mother's lifetime habit of daily Scripture reading. Nor have many in our churches. But I wonder what we might be losing in the process.

I do not raise this question as a lead in to a 'Back to Basics' campaign. I don't believe that it would be right, either for children or for adults, to go back to the mindless, repetitive way Scripture was once taught. But I do find myself wondering just what we *are* doing, in place of the numbing repetition, to internalise Scripture. The old methods may have rightly been discredited. But what new methods are we using in their place? If there are none, is this because it is no longer a priority to *ingest* the word of God? If so, and this may be a deeply unfashionable assertion, I wonder if our faith might be the weaker for it.

Internalising the faith, getting it deeper than the intellect, into the very DNA of our mindset and motivations, is in part about letting God's story shape us. And to do that we have to know it; to be exposed to it in all its richness and diversity; to be moved by its poetry; puzzled by its prophecies; stirred by its history; confused, perhaps, by its complexity. We have to become *intentional*, like the pro-book protestors of *Fahrenheit 451*, in our efforts to get God's story under our skin.

Perhaps we are not all in a position to ingest the whole breadth of Scripture. Perhaps 'the Bible in a year' for many of us is more realistically 'the Bible in roughly twenty years': but the issue is as much one of quality as of quantity. Barry

Taylor, former AC/DC roadie and now an unorthodox church-planter in Los Angeles, illustrates the principle well. Often when speaking at Christian events he explains how hard he finds it to let Scripture really sink in to his life. As a result he has made a determined decision to get at least *some* of the Scripture deeply into his being. 'And this is the part I am working on at the moment', he will say, as he takes a single page of the Bible out of his pocket. He is reading the Bible one page at a time, and each page will travel with him, carried in his pocket until he really thinks

The deeper it goes, the more it will shape us

he has 'got it', at which point another page can be torn, folded and carried – perhaps for a day, perhaps a month. It is an unusual approach and for some perhaps controversial, but it has this in its favour: it is a determined effort. What might it take for you to get Scripture *into your bones?* Whether a verse at a time, a page at a time or a book at a time, the principle is the same – the deeper it goes, the more it will shape us.

Henri Nouwen, when praying for several months in the silence of a Trappist monastery, discovered in the memorisation and repetition of the Psalms a source of incomparable strength and sustenance. He said of the poetry of these ancient words

> … slowly these words enter into the centre of my heart. They are more real than ideas, images, comparisons: they become a real presence. … Many times I have thought if I am ever sent to prison, if I am ever subjected to hunger, pain, torture or humiliation, I hope and pray that they let me keep the Psalms. … How happy are those who no longer need books but carry the Psalms in their heart wherever they are and wherever they go.[21]

God²go

The ultimate failure of Nebuchadnezzar's programme of assimilation, and the victory of Daniel's intrinsic faith, is demonstrated in a minor textual detail recorded in Daniel 5:12. In this later chapter, twenty-three years have passed since the death of Nebuchadnezzar, (described here as Belshazzar's 'father' in the sense of predecessor rather than of biological parent). Daniel, around eighty at the time, is not part of Belshazzar's immediate staff; but when help is needed to interpret the writing on the wall, it is the Queen (almost certainly Belshazzar's mother, rather than his wife) who remembers Daniel and his strange gifts. Her description of him to Belshazzar is remarkable. He is 'Daniel, whom the king called Belteshazzar' (Dan. 5:12). This is a reference to Nebuchadnezzar's decision sixty years earlier, at the very outset of Daniel's exile, that new names would be given to the exiles (Dan. 1:7). In the case of Shadrach, Meshach and Abednego (formerly Hananiah, Mishael and Azariah), it is by these new, Babylonian names that they are referred to in the text and that we remember them today. But not so Daniel. After over sixty years of attempted assimilation, Daniel is still referred to by his Hebrew name and this is at the highest level of royal power – by the Queen herself. He has kept his identity and integrity.

The king of Babylon gave Daniel a new name but Babylon has not given him a new identity. Daniel is as Daniel was: his own person and Yahweh's servant. For all the awesome power of Babylon, the power of God at work in Daniel's life has proved stronger. An intrinsic faith, an inner strength that does not depend on external props for its survival, has enabled Daniel to come through the most sophisticated programme of assimilation in the known world of his day with his identity intact.

The great secret of the text of Daniel, the priceless jewel at its heart, the explosive discovery Daniel makes and delivers to all Israel, is this – that God himself is not fazed by the losses of exile. Daniel's God, it turns out, is not too small for Babylon, but too big. He is victorious, he is in control, he is committed to fulfilling his plans; he is there for Israel. All these things are true, but not on the small scale with which the Hebrews had formerly measured such things. Rather, it is on a global scale that God is sovereign. It is as the universal king that he reigns. He is bigger, in Daniel, than the biggest human ruler: more powerful than the most powerful dictator. The loss of the temple doesn't throw him because he is so much bigger than the temple. The invasion of the land does not stop him because he has plans for the whole earth. The exile does not distance him from his people because there is nowhere they can go where he will not be found.

Daniel discovers that Yahweh is a 'God^{2}Go' – a take-away God who travels with you wherever you are taken. Daniel's faith is a portable faith – a pocket-sized power-pack that can be carried into every circumstance and connect with God's mainframe from any portal. Exile does not faze Daniel, because it has not fazed his God. Temple worship was great and encouraging, and doubtless Daniel missed it as much as those who later hung their harps mournfully on Babylon's riverside trees, refusing to sing the Lord's song. But Daniel was not *dependent* on the temple. He could worship God wherever he was: surrounded by countless crowds of strange and even hostile pagans; knowing that the great monuments of Nebuchadnezzar's great city pointed not to Yahweh but to other, lesser gods; under pressure and under fire; trapped in a strange land a long way from home. Nor was Daniel limited to being located in Jerusalem; or to serving God's anointed king over

Israel. Royalty; temple-worship; civic life – all these Daniel missed but on none of them was he *dependent*. He did not need the visible victory of God to trust in God's promises. His *internalised* faith turned out, in the event, to be stronger and more lasting than any *externalised* faith relying on the trappings of Jerusalem worship.

He did not need the visible victory of God to trust in God's promises

Jim Wallis suggests that it is this kind of faith that changes the world

> Hebrew 11:1 says that faith is 'the substance of things hoped for and the evidence of things not seen'. The world is waiting for a people who will offer the value of hope. Hope that change is possible. Hope that inspires them to bet their lives on such change. My own paraphrase of Hebrews 11:1 is this: *Hope is believing in spite of the evidence, and then watching the evidence change...*[22]

s t r e t c hing exercises

Intrinsic faith

What is the difference, for you, between an internal and an external faith? If the props were taken away, would your faith remain strong? Is there a difference, for you, between the legitimate props on which you are called to lean (Scripture; the love and support of fellow believers; an active life of worship) and other props you have taken on that become a substitute for God's own work in your life?

Pray for the discernment to know the right balance between an externally supported and an internally grounded faith. Ask God if there are 'props' that you should try to live without. Ask him, above all, to so deepen and strengthen your inner life that you carry the fire of faith in your very bones.

Faith in C-Minor

Take a moment to reflect on the difference it makes to view faith as a performance in a major or minor key. Are there ways in which you have lived in a major key that might now be changing? What difference might it make to your church's engagement with its community if you were to go through a 'key shift' in your approach?

Pray that God would give you the right approach for every situation. Where gentleness is needed, pray for the gentle gift of God's mercy. Where confidence is needed, pray for certain faith. Pray for all those in your community who, for whatever reason, have never heard God's song – ask God how best his song might be performed for them to hear it.

Scripture

Consider the role that Scripture plays in your life. Do you need to dive more deeply into God's word? Do you need to create more regular routines with which to ingest Scripture? Is the challenge before you to go *wider* – reading more of God's word, or to go *deeper* – letting a small part of God's word get into your bones each day? Whichever your need is, reflect on Scripture and what changes you might make to 'eat God's story' more fully and consistently.

Pray for a moment about any area of concern you have identified or any commitment you have made. Ask God to give you a realistic, human-scale strategy for allowing his story to shape your life more richly and deeply.

CHAPTER TWO

acoustic

Daniel replied, 'No wise man, enchanter, magician or diviner can explain to the king the mystery he has asked about, but there is a God in heaven who reveals mysteries' (Dan. 2:27,28).

acoustic, –al, *adj.* Pertaining to the sense of hearing or to the theory of sounds: used in hearing, auditory: operated by sound vibrations, as an acoustic mine... *Chambers Dictionary*[23]

acoustic faith: faith grounded in the learned art of listening

Foot, mouth and ears...

Shortly after the recent Foot and Mouth crisis had swept through the UK, destroying lives and livelihoods as it moved, I was invited by a friend in the advertising industry to view a collection of award-winning commercials. Among these was an excellent short piece publicising the work of the Samaritans, whose counsellors had been hugely involved in helping people brought to their knees by the impact of this disease. Pieced together from genuine news footage and interviews recorded during the crisis, the advert presents the pain felt by those who were seeing their livestock destroyed and the carcasses burned. I use this commercial regularly in seminars and lectures and have thus watched it perhaps

> There is something disarmingly powerful about hearing people tell their own story

thirty times but it has the power to move me every time. There is something disarmingly powerful about hearing people tell their own story and allowing their struggles to get under your skin.

What struck me as I first viewed this harrowing piece of communication was that I had not, until that point, truly listened to those impacted by this crisis. I had lived through the entire saga in the UK; I had participated as a church leader in events in which we prayed for those affected; I had read and heard reports of their plight. But like many others I had followed the media lead in making the glaringly inaccurate assumption about these people that their primary concern was money. It was because they were facing financial ruin, we were told, that the farming community were so distressed by the Foot and Mouth epidemic. Watching on-screen interviews with those same farmers changed my view. I saw that something much deeper was happening; that for someone who has worked all their lives with animals, the mass culls of cattle were more than an economic event. For some of these people this was the single most traumatic incident they had lived through and nothing would ever be the same.

I tell this story because it illustrates something very important for me in our exploration of faith in exile. I had lived in the same universe as these people throughout their trauma, but I had frankly neither truly heard them nor truly cared. My response, as a city-dweller, to the Foot and Mouth reports was sympathetic but misguided. I hadn't properly responded because I hadn't properly understood. And this, in turn, was because I hadn't properly *listened*. It took the imagination and inspiration of the Samaritans, the skills of a professional advertising agency and the artful use of editing and music to get me to hear what I had missed. In order to truly engage with a given cultural setting, you have to learn, before all else, to listen.

I believe that the life of Daniel shows a remarkable capacity to listen and that this is the driving force of his famous prophetic gifting. *He is stretched between the tasks of listening on the one hand to the voice of God and on the other to the voices of the culture in which he finds himself living.* We are used to saying that Daniel, by the grace and gifting of

Yahweh, was able to hear the word of God and pass it on to those around him, not least to the kings of Babylon – and we tend to categorise this as an entirely spiritual, other-worldly gift. But prophecy can never be so one-sided: it is a bridge between two worlds. Daniel would not have been able to speak the prophetic word of God into his culture and context unless he had already been prepared to immerse himself in listening to that culture. From the first moments of his exile, he exhibits a willingness to listen – to engage fully with Babylon. He catches the rhythms of the city. He hears the whisper of its need. In his dealings with Nebuchadnezzar, there is evidence that he has deeply understood the king's condition and longings. He speaks God's word into a situation he has grasped. Like an artiste who knows his audience, his performance is tinged with a wisdom born of 'double-listening' – one ear open to the God who speaks to men and women, and the other to the men and women to whom God will speak. Daniel does not pronounce disembodied truths, hovering above their context and failing to find an earthing point. Rather, he speaks, on God's behalf, words well-aimed to reach the heart of the exact person to whom they are addressed. Daniel's tongue is prophetically anointed but so, it seems, are his ears.

He catches the rhythms of the city

What Dreams May Come

Daniel 2 is set in the early years of the exile and describes Daniel's first high-profile 'engagement' with King Nebuchadnezzar. The king has been disturbed by a vivid dream. Clearly it should mean something, but he doesn't know what and all the wise men of Babylon can't tell him. The king, who holds the power of life and death over all his subjects, decrees that all the wise men will be killed unless an interpreter is found. This brings Daniel and his friends into the story, as Daniel takes the lead in averting certain death. Through prayer, he is able to discern both the dream and its meaning, and he delivers this to the king. The interpretation catapults Daniel's prophetic role to centre stage, because the dream proves to be a direct message from God for the king concerning the future of his reign. So convinced is Nebuchadnezzar of the interpretation offered that he pours honour on Daniel and his friends and acknowledges Yahweh as 'God of gods'.

It is in the course of this episode that the 'wisdom and tact' of Daniel is noted. Here is an individual whose decisions and declarations are dripping with the anointing of God in the everyday as much as in the spectacular. Listening for the voice of God, whether it comes to him through Scripture, through intuition and observation or through the strange dream of a pagan king, Daniel lives in optimum openness: reaching out for God's word for his situation. It is this gift, this anointed double-listening, that propels Daniel to prominence in Babylon and ultimately leads to the conversion of the king.

> Whatever reason we give, the concluding scene gives us a powerful picture that reinforces the theme of our book: the most powerful pagan in the world lies prostrate before an exiled Jew. Chills of excitement and the flames of hope will rise in the hearts of those who identify with Daniel and his God.[24]

Acoustic faith is a faith grounded in double-listening, a faith that can discern the whisper of God in the culture – at once affirming and judging; questioning and answering; pointing the way to fullness of life. This is the faith that will carry us through whatever Babylons we must live in; that will strengthen us whatever changes come. This is faith that, by virtue of its interactive nature, is able to meet, understand and do business with every cultural setting and people group.

When I was growing up in Bath through the 1970s, one of the more effective local Christians was a man called Bob Holman. Bob has gone on to become a well-known writer and speaker on social issues and to develop projects of great significance on the notorious Easterhouse estate in Glasgow. But in the early 1970s he was a lecturer in Sociology at Bath University. He was aware, both as a sociologist and as a Christian, that despite the great wealth of the city of Bath, there were large estates whose people experienced genuine social poverty. One of these, the Whiteway Estate, was plagued by youth crime and housed many families who were experiencing real difficulties but couldn't seem to 'connect' with whatever help was available from the local council or social services.

Bob decided that something could and should be done and that the answer lay in an incarnational model of Christian ministry. He reduced his lecturing hours to part-time and rented a house on the Whiteway Estate. As a result of this decision, over the ensuing years, a number of dramatic changes took place. A church was planted. A community centre was built. Local people became the leaders of both. A nationally significant 'Neighbourhood Project' was founded. My good friend Dave Wiles came out of the local drugs scene to become a Christian, then to qualify as a social worker and, in good time, to become the National Director of the Frontier Youth Trust.

The most significant link in this chain of events was the first. It was the initial action that Bob Holman took as a new resident of the Whiteway Estate that made all the difference. And it was a simple, unpretentious act: he left his kitchen door open. At the outset, this was his only act of mission. He left his door open and he let people know, as time went on, that he was there to help them if they needed help. He listened. He helped where he could. Massive changes grew from that small act, like the flap of a butterfly's wing changing a whole climate. Bob very quickly became a trusted member of the community, and through his knowledge, resources and contacts he was able to help many of his neighbours: even to the point that the youth crime statistics for the area took a measurable nose-dive. His first act was not one of power but of powerlessness. He did not become anyone's saviour. He became many people's friend: in their time and on their terms. He loved through listening.

The most significant link in this chain of events was the first

The gospel that Bob Holman had come to love and understand is a gospel that neither asks for nor needs the pomp and power of social superiority. It is a gospel that does not meet a new cultural situation with conquering and crusading zeal. Rather, it wins people's trust by deeply, genuinely and substantially loving them. And love begins with listening.

A Virtual Verona

What is true of individuals can also be true of a wider culture. We demonstrate the incarnational love of Christ by being willing to listen and learn. The film that most captured my attention in the late 1990s was, without doubt, Baz Luhrmann's flamboyant *William Shakespeare's Romeo and Juliet.* Starring Leonardo DiCaprio and Clare Danes, this youthful adaptation of 'the greatest love story of all time' swapped Shakespeare's Verona for a fictional 'Verona Beach' to weave together a futuristic tale of love, rivalry, drugs and crime against a soundtrack featuring some of the biggest recording artists of the day. I watched the film on separate occasions with each of my (then) teenage children, and was struck each time by the level of their 'connection' with this story and by the extent to which my own understanding of the original play was deepened.

The central device of Luhrmann's film is that his actors speak Shakespeare's original words. Other than some subtle editing and the occasionally repeated line, the script of the film is the script of the play. But here the continuity ends: every other aspect of this production – from scenes and settings via costumes and characterisations to props and production values – is a radical departure from any previous version of the play. Like a Dr Who of the literary scene, Luhrmann takes a time-travel machine to sweep up one of the world's best-loved plays and drop it into the post-modern world. With visual references to every decade from the 1960s to the 1990s, and copious allusions to such cinema classics as James Dean's *Rebel Without A Cause*, the film is a frame-by-frame explosion of teen culture. And the technique works. When the prologue is presented as a TV News Report, content and context meet with astounding communicative power. The same is true in Pete Postlethwaite's incarnation of Father Laurence and Vondie Curtis-Hall's 'Captain Prince': both bring an ancient language into a contemporary context to uncanny effect. The story comes newly alive as its inner nuances are projected onto a contemporary screen.

I value this film as perhaps the most potent recent expression of the task to which the people of God are called in every time and culture through which they pass. Luhrmann's commitment to the original script is fuelled neither by dull conformity nor by mere sentiment. He believes – he *knows* – that Shakespeare's story has the power to move a new generation. His job as director is not to change the story in

His job as director is not to change the story

order that it might be relevant; it is to unlock its inner power in new ways. Contextualisation neither adds to nor subtracts from the story but it gives the story the best possible opportunity to speak in a new setting. Luhrmann is, by definition, a double-listener. He has listened to Shakespeare, discerning every detail and nuance of a complex emotional adventure; finding the heart and soul of a timeless tale. And he has listened to the culture: finding the points of connection, pitching a voice that will be heard.

Thus was Daniel called in Babylon, not to 'update' the story of Yahweh to make God more palatable to pagans, but to discern points of contact. How might an ambitious king, who sees himself at the epicentre of global history, be persuaded of the sovereignty of God? How does Jerusalem's Yahweh speak on the streets of Babylon? What riches are there, in the ancient tales of the Hebrew journey, to fund its interaction with a world made strange? Daniel must be driven both by *faithfulness* and by *improvisation*; his is an ancient-future faith, true both to the 'oldness' of God's story and to the 'newness' of this context.

And thus are we called, in every changing culture, to find a landing place for God's kingdom. To be prophetic is to be stretched between ideas and their implementation, between the content of God's message and its context. It is to be acoustic: always listening; always looking both ways.

This is the faith expressed by theologian Jurgen Moltmann as the core of the church's calling in society

> The church will always have to present itself both in the forum of God and in the forum of the world. For it stands for God to the world, and it stands for the world before God. It confronts the world in critical liberty and is bound to give it the authentic revelation of the new life. At the same time it stands before God in fellowship and solidarity with all men and is bound to send up to him out of the depths the common cry for life and liberty.[25]

It is the faith expressed in the life and creativity of actor Rob Lacey, author of the remarkable *The Word on the Street*:[26] a contemporary and creative re-imagining of the biblical text. Through the three years that it took Rob to complete the writing of this important text, he faced the very real possibility of dying. He was fairly recently married, with a young son, Lukas, and experienced a battle with cancer that took him to the very threshold of death: to the point at which his doctors advised him to 'settle his affairs' and say goodbye to his friends and family. He endured long periods in which it was impossible to work for even a few minutes a day. He struggled with the strange possibility that the God he was so determined to know and make known might, after all, abandon him to tragedy and terror. Yet he pressed on and wrestled with the story of God and what it might mean for today's complex world.

The song of the exiles in Psalm 137 is rendered with authentic passion and anger

The result is a text which is not only creative and funny, lucid and perceptive, but is also touched with something deeper. This is especially true in the Psalms, where Rob revisits the words of others who, before him, have asked why the God who loves them so much seems to have abandoned them so terribly. The song of the exiles in Psalm 137 is rendered with authentic passion and anger

The Babylon rivers flowed along,
But our tears nearly broke their banks;
Our hearts were wading in the rivers back home,
Our instruments dumb in this depression zone;
And what? They expected us to sing our songs?
These slave drivers request our party songs!

And Psalm 23, the hymn that speaks so eloquently of trust in the face of fear, takes on new depth

You're with me, and you comfort me.
You're my guide and my guard, my minder, my mentor.
What more do I need, what's better at the centre?
You sit me down, put my best CD on,
My soul remembers who I am again.
You call me to the streets, you show me such good things,
Right things with no hidden strings, just your name on,
And it's game on,
And your great repute, like a distant flute, it comforts me.
You're with me, and you comfort me.
As I crawl through the alley of the shadow of cancer
I know you know the answer,
And the battle won't rattle me:
You're around, and I've found your empathy,
Your symphony of sympathy that comforts me.
You lay out a table, you sit me down.

My rivals arrive from the greatest to the least,
But my cup's kept full and my head's held high,
And you boast about me, your least priest
You make them toast me, right through the feast.
Boy, does it comfort me,
You're with me, and you comfort me.

The *Word on the Street* is more than just a clever, contemporary rendition of Scripture. It is a powerful text forged in the author's own valley of suffering. It brings the story of God alive in our confusing and complex world because it is written by someone who has opened himself to that very confusion and complexity: who has allowed the pain of the world to touch him. Without this openness, both to the Spirit of God and to the whisper of the world, it would not have half its power. Love is listening.

God is a DJ

In a hard-hitting exploration of ethnic identity called *Castrating Culture*, theologian Dewi Hughes speaks of the impact on his life of meeting a humble tribal leader from a remote area of Peru, Artidoro Tuanama. Artidoro is the director of the Association of Quechua Evangelical Churches of the Jungle, based in north-east Peru. Dewi Hughes writes

> … His people continue to live most of their lives outside the boundaries of industrialisation and globalisation. They are not numerous. In global terms, and relative to the numerous and powerful nations of the earth, they count for nothing. A very sophisticated electronic scale would be required to even register their existence – for all the great nations of the earth,

with their splendour, glory and power, are but dust on God's scales. Before God, the might and longevity of all the nations appear as nothing (Isaiah 40:15-17).

This may be so, but Artidoro has also understood something of the genius of the gospel with its revelation of a God who 'has brought down rulers from their thrones but has lifted up the humble ... has filled the hungry with good things but has sent the rich away empty' (Luke 1:52-53). He has understood that, having welcomed the gospel, his little people by the world's standards have a responsibility to live out the gospel in the context of their history and culture.[27]

The controversial title of Dewi Hughes' book is taken from a statement made by Artidoro that captures his passion for the Christian gospel and for his people

We simply want to take our place as indigenous and native Quechua people, understanding and living out the gospel. We assume our identity without shame, retaliation or indignation against those who have caused harm to our past and castrated our culture.[28]

Dewi Hughes cites this example to illustrate the importance, in God's sight, of even the smallest and least significant of human cultures but it serves to illustrate a deeper truth still: that faith can never be 'pure' and other-worldly. It is always contextualised. God speaks into human cultures because it is in human cultures that the miracle of the gospel will be displayed. Faith is a conversation between earth and heaven, between the human and the divine. New Zealander Steve Taylor, who has recently completed a PhD research programme exploring issues of faith and mission in post-modern culture, uses the powerful image of God as a DJ. In communicating with us, he suggests, God takes and samples the sounds and voices of a culture and, with them, weaves something new. There is no pure 'Christian' culture, because every expression of faith and church is, by

> **Faith is a conversation between earth and heaven**

definition, a godly re-mix of human cultures. The recipe may be God's and the result Spirit-inspired, but the ingredients are human, through and through.

Prophetic ministry, in this understanding, is defined not solely as speaking God's words into a culture, but as double-listening. Prophets are willing to offer their lives as a bridge between the reality of heaven and the culture and context in which they live. Every plane must have a landing place. Incarnation is specific. Jesus did not just become human; he became *a* human, born into the blood and straw of a particular time and place. Every people group and culture, in the biblical terminology every *ethnie*, is waiting for the double-listening prophets who will earth the glories of heaven in their specific time and place. This is the role for which Artidoro Tuanama has volunteered among the Quechua Indians. It is the role given in Babylon to Daniel: to speak God's word into the specific context of a pagan regime and to take his double-listening to the very heart and centre of that regime, the royal palace. To do this he had no choice but to listen in both directions. His early years in Babylon were those of a doctor, holding a stethoscope against the heart of a culture: listening for every murmur. Viv Thomas captures this sense of cultural immersion in his book *Second Choice*, a creative and compelling exploration of Daniel's life

> God's people were called to live in Babylon in a context
> dominated by superstition, omens and fear. Daniel and his
> Hebrew friends responded to this by embracing Babylon in
> every way possible, consistent with their responsibility to
> God. They chose to live their faith and yet be integrated
> into the heavily contaminated world of Babylon. So, in the
> embrace of their second-choice world they affirmed that it
> was not Nebuchadnezzar, Belshazzar or Darius who was in
> control … but God.[29]

This is why I am moved when I listen to Eminem, or read an interview with Marilyn Manson. This is why I am fascinated by the queues waiting to hand over their hard-earned wages to watch *Eternal Sunshine of the Spotless Mind* or *Lost in Translation*: not only for what these artists and films have to say in themselves, but for what they have to say *about* those who listen so raptly to them. This is why, in the confusion and cacophony of the post-modern world, the marketing slogan of Luhrmann's *Moulin Rouge* so grips me, 'The greatest thing that you can learn is just to love and to be loved in return': this single phrase captures so powerfully the longings of a lost generation. The late Joe Strummer went down in history at the height of the punk revolution for saying that he was 'doing it for the kids' and it was true. Punk could never have happened, just as Elvis a generation earlier would never have been discovered, if there wasn't a generation waiting, just waiting for someone to put their feelings into words.

A Mars Hill a day

A powerful New Testament example of this same double-listening is given in Acts 17. The apostle Paul is temporarily grounded in the midst of a preaching tour while he waits in Athens for his travelling companions to join him. Perhaps this respite was God-arranged, forcing the great activist to slow down for a while, but whatever its cause, its effect was clear: Paul used the time to *look and listen*. He wandered the great city of Athens, increasingly astounded, disturbed and intrigued by what he saw. As he visited shrine after shrine in the

Paul used the time to *look and listen*

city's countless places of worship, he began to get under the skin of idolatry, to understand not only what was happening but why it was happening and to sense the questions it left unanswered. The result was that by the time Paul did have opportunity to speak, he did so from a perspective of understanding and sympathy. The platform from which he preached was shaped by his listening. This process is starkly illustrated by two verses. In Acts 17:16 we are told that Paul was 'greatly distressed to see that the city was full of idols'. Just a few days later, when he stands on Mars Hill and at last has the opportunity to address a pagan audience, his mood seems to have changed.

> 'Men of Athens!' he says, 'I see that in every way you are very religious. For as I walked around and looked carefully at your objects of worship, I even found an altar with this inscription: TO AN UNKNOWN GOD. Now what you worship as something unknown I am going to proclaim to you.'[30]

I want to suggest that this model has huge significance for the changing times in which we find ourselves. It is no coincidence that Acts 17 is a deeply resonant passage for many pursuing Christian mission in a post-modern, post-Christendom generation. They see in it not only a parallel with the rampant pluralism and spiritual searching of their peers, but also a response that has integrity, authenticity and currency for our times. The challenge is acute for those who engage in the activity we call *evangelism*. Because we associate evangelism with proclamation, and use verbs such as 'telling', 'sharing', 'speaking' and 'preaching', we see the primary skills of the evangelist in terms of the outward flow of communication.

The challenge is acute for those who engage in the activity we call *evangelism*

It is those best able to express themselves who are most readily appointed, in our churches, to this task. But Paul clearly learned in Athens the same lesson Daniel learned in Babylon: that the evangelist is given ears to hear as well a mouth to speak. The message 'hits home' when it has been forged in listening, the longings and aspirations of the culture giving shape to the message that emerges. Like the bards of ancient Celtic culture, prophets speak both *into* and *out of* the culture: they are interpreters of history as well as actors within it.

Can we learn to make *listening* a primary aspect of our evangelistic ministries? Are we prepared to release those gifted as listeners, as well as those gifted to speak, into this crucial task? Are we willing to let our interaction with contemporary culture – whether it is the Foot and Mouth crisis or the colourful language of Eminem – be shaped by our need to learn rather than our desire to judge? The truly anointed evangelist, I believe, is not the person who loves the gospel so passionately that they cannot help sharing it with people: it is the person who loves people so passionately that they cannot but want the best for them. I admit to having met evangelists who don't even seem to *like* people very much, let alone love them. I'm not sure if this is sustainable in a biblical view of mission. Our listening should be born out of genuine engagement with culture and a genuine fascination with people: nothing less will be pure or strong enough to build a platform for our gospel.

To adopt this approach is to recognise that listening is both a gift and a learned activity. It is a gift in the sense that God gives to us the capacity to hear the cry of the human heart. Empathy, the ability to see, hear and understand the situation in which another person lives, is one of the characteristics that makes us human. It is a gift from our Creator. Like all gifts, some seem to 'have it' more than others. But it is also a learned activity. We can take the gift that God gives and develop it. We can learn to listen more fully, more deeply. Like every God-given gift, the gift of listening can be strengthened or stifled; worked on or wasted. It can be an activity we value and nurture and give time and attention to, or it can be an inconvenience we would rather avoid.

For my own part, it is a gift I need and am committed to seeking. I am not a 'born listener'. The communication skills I seem to have are more often associated with speaking and writing. When I am in a room full of people with my wife she will, more often than not, see and hear things that I totally miss. As we talk later, she will reflect care and concern for someone whose needs I hadn't even noticed. But I have seen enough of the operation and effectiveness of listening to know how much it matters. May God deliver us from 'answering before listening'.[31]

Resident aliens

The confidence, faith and energy with which we listen come from the life-changing affirmation that, for all its faults, it is ultimately God's world we are listening to. In the New Testament, the metaphor closest to Daniel's experience of exile is that of 'resident aliens'. This is the concept used both in Hebrews (Heb.11:13) and in the letters of Peter (1 Pet. 2:11), and is a complex image of a people who are both 'at home' and 'far from home' in the world, both residents and strangers in every culture in which God places them. The concept has gained currency recently, as theologians and missiologists explore the sense of exile as applicable to Christian life in a post-Christian culture. It is a concept, however, that is misunderstood by the church whenever an 'other-worldly' theology convinces believers that they have no place at all in this world: that their true home is elsewhere.

One of the images that is often used to capture the sense of *resident aliens* is that of an expatriate community – familiar to those who have travelled in the Middle East, where whole armies of western workers have established a life as 'resident aliens'. Expatriates, by definition, are shaped by the sense that *life* is here, but *home* is somewhere else. 'This is where I live and work: but it is not my home.' Very often their lives are dominated by nostalgia for that 'somewhere else' and by the attempt to surround themselves with the trappings of home. The status of 'resident alien' to an expatriate is a statement about being away from home: and for most there is the promise of return. Home is the 'elsewhere' that I come from, that I long for and that one day I will see again. But this image is a false rendering of the biblical 'resident aliens', and it touches on one of the deepest ways in which the contemporary church has missed the meaning of exile. We may experience exile in the cultures of Babylon, but the deeper reality of the gospel tells us that we are *at home on planet earth*. There is no elsewhere. This *is* home.

Daniel is a stranger in Babylon and in that sense he is away from home. But in another, much deeper sense, he is at home; because Babylon is still part of God's world. The earth on which it stands is God's earth. This contrasts to some extent with the longing for a home that is reflected in the lament of Psalm 137. The exiles long for a home that is elsewhere. Nostalgia is their daily fare – and 'return' is the only promise they can bear to hold onto. Life is here but home is somewhere else. We will see in a later chapter that this honest embracing of lament – this readiness to name and know the devastation God has wrought; this willingness to mourn – is a right and proper response to the trauma and dislocation of exile. The psalmists are right to grieve. But as the text of Daniel insists, they are wrong about Babylon. They assume that this land that is foreign to them is also foreign to their God. They can't sing God's songs *here* because this is not God's land. The secret they have not yet discovered, the truth they do not know, is that *Babylon is God's*. Their God is, as Daniel and the later prophets of exile affirm, the *God of all creation*; the *God of all history* and the *God of all peoples*.[32]

> **But in another, much deeper sense, he is at home**

This terrible event, this deportation of the people from Jerusalem to Babylon, *is God's idea* (Dan.1:2). This is perhaps the strangest assertion of the book of Daniel but is also its most important. For Daniel, it all happens as part of God's reign. The evil emperor Nebuchadnezzar, who has ripped the people from their land and taken them as captives to his city, was given his power *by the God of heaven* (Dan. 2:37). Belshazzar, who as Prince Regent inherits the absolute power of the earlier emperor but adds to it his own twist of pride and cruelty, is bluntly told about the God 'who holds in his hand your life and all your ways' (Dan. 5:23). The Persian king Cyrus, who later conquers Babylon and decrees that the Hebrew exiles can finally begin to return home, does all this *as God's shepherd*, whose right hand God himself holds (Is. 44:28 and 45:1). These are powerful people, who worship foreign gods and rule in foreign lands: but none of them is outside the scope of God's reign. He is the God of the whole earth and Babylon, as much as Jerusalem, is on his turf.

This important distinction, so sadly misunderstood by the musicians of Psalm 137 but so powerfully grasped by Daniel and the prophets of exile, marks a growth moment in the theology of Israel. It is this post-exilic theology, not the earlier version in which God could only rule in Jerusalem, that sets the tone for the New Testament concept of *resident aliens*. We are not aliens because our home is elsewhere but because our inheritance has not yet been revealed. The place we live and work in *is* our home. It *is* our destiny and our inheritance. We are aliens in it now, for the time being, because Babylon, on a provisional basis and within the unfolding plan of the sovereign God, has been allowed to establish its illegitimate, temporary and unsustainable empire on God's turf.

It is Babylon, not planet earth, that is foreign to us. The idea popularised in the 1970s through Larry Norman's album title *Only Visiting This Planet*, carried in Hal Lindsay's

> **We are not aliens because our home is elsewhere**

equally popular book *The Late Great Planet Earth* and to some extent re-invented for the blockbuster *Left Behind* series, is a false reading of the concept of resident aliens. It is not on planet earth that we live as strangers but in the proud cities that idolatrous humanity has fashioned here. The land we seek, the land that is held for us in promise, is there beneath our feet. The promise of God is buried deep in the soil over which we walk – hidden from our sight because too much has been built over it. It is the clamour of the city, the pride and power of Babylon, the sex and selling and stridency of the market-place that drowns out the call home.

This is why it is so crucial that we read what is actually written in Scripture, rather than what we expect to find. In the letter to the Hebrews, for example, we are encouraged to emulate the faith of Abraham, who responded to the call of God to live in the world 'like a stranger in a foreign country' in anticipation of God's promise. But where exactly did he live?

> By faith Abraham, when called to go to a place he would later receive as his inheritance, obeyed and went, even though he did not know where he was going. By faith he made his home in the promised land like a stranger in a foreign country; he lived in tents, as did Isaac and Jacob, who were heirs with him of the same promise. For he was looking forward to the city with foundations, whose architect and builder is God (Heb. 11:8-10).

Abraham was called *to* the place he would later receive as his inheritance; he went in obedience to God's call and even when he got there, he lived as a stranger *in the very place* God had promised. With every step that Abraham took, his foot fell on soil that God had sworn to give him. It was in the land of promise that he lived as a stranger, and it would be in the land of promise that the city 'whose architect and builder is God' would be founded.

The measure of Abraham's faith was not that he was able to live as a foreigner in one place, knowing that he belonged in another: it was that he was able be live *as a stranger in the land that was promised to him*. He trusted God's promise – even though the rising of the sun each day brought to light the incontrovertible evidence that the land was not his, that the promise was not fulfilled. He trusted the promise even though every field and well he passed on his journeying, every town and city he visited, every wall and roof and tower and dome spoke

This land is ours, not God's'

not of the presence of Yahweh but of his absence. Before his eyes were the structures and the systems, the buildings and beliefs that screamed 'this land is ours, not God's', but *underneath his feet* was the soil of the land he had been promised. The future to which God's people are called in Scripture is not a future in which they are whisked away from an earthly experience to live forever in a better place. It is a future in which God's rule comes to earth; in which the tatty and temporary rule of Babylon is once and for all brought down; in which the very cosmos is made new and the creation rejoices in the healing, redeeming touch of its Creator's love. We are resident aliens in Babylon because we are waiting for the ultimate consummation of God's plan, when John's visionary cry of triumph will be *our* song, ringing out through actual history, in the reality of a cosmos made new

> Now the dwelling of God is with men, and he will live with them. They will be his people, and God himself will be with them and be their God. He will wipe every tear from

their eyes. There will be no more death or mourning or crying or pain, for the old order of things has passed away.[33]

Babylon is not offensive to God because it is built on ground outside of his care and concern: it is offensive to God because it is built on *his* ground. Every billboard that shouts out 'image is our god'; every high-rise that proclaims money's triumph; every skyline whose very outline is a hymn of praise to human greatness; every symbol of the pride and power of Adam's children cries out against the truth that the earth is God's. But the promise remains. The days of conceit and clamour are numbered; the city's ultimate destruction is assured because God has whispered to the universe, in words that the loudest symphony cannot drown: 'the meek shall inherit the earth.'

It is precisely because we are 'at home' in God's earth – God's made-good, covenant-ruled, blood-redeemed planet – that we are strangers in Babylon. It is Babylon that is only visiting this planet.

This distinction matters to us because it will deeply shape the way we view the world we live in. If our home is 'elsewhere', we have little need to be involved and engaged in the concerns of this present world. But if this *is* our home, temporarily held by the occupying forces of Babylon, then we will be called to a 'deep listening': a listening that tries to hear, under and beyond the loud cry of Babylon, the whisper of God in *his* world.

Transforming presence

This conviction empowers us to be a transforming presence in our world. Though we live as resident aliens in this world, it is God's world we live in. God's promised future is coming, even though we may not see it now, and as surely as grass grows under our feet though we don't see it growing, so the seeds of the kingdom are taking root and moving inexorably towards their fulfilment. Because we know what the future holds; because we have read the closing pages of the book and know who wins; because the question'Whose earth is it anyway?' is answered for us: we can walk through every Babylon God throws us into, holding onto a faith that *changes* the very road it travels on.

There is a verse is Psalm 84 that lodged itself in my brain many years ago and has sung its song to me ever since. It describes the faith of those who interact with their circumstances but are not destroyed by them.'As they pass through the Valley of Baca', it sings, 'they make it a place of springs'.[34] The Valley of Baca is not known as a real place in the Old Testament and is generally assumed to be a symbolic location. The context suggests a

They transform these same valleys into 'a place of springs'

desert road and the etymology of 'Baca'points to a'place of weeping'. The image, then, is of a group of pilgrims whose journey takes them through dry places of affliction. But these pilgrims are not forced by such places into dryness themselves: rather they transform these same valleys into'a place of springs'. These are people who put more into the world than they take out of it; people whose inner wells of faith are full enough to feed the faith of others. These are people who make more of a dent on their culture than their culture makes on them. They are 'present' to the culture – they are there in the place of dryness and tears – but they lift it, somehow, to higher aspirations.

I believe that people who know where the world is going, who have a deep, inner sense of the plans of God, can greatly influence those around them. They can show a confidence and courage that does nor come from circumstances, but from their faith in God. It is strange indeed to pass through a world of disaster, disturbance and disease and yet to cling to hope. But if you *know* that the destiny of that same world is to be transformed by the love of its Creator, and that its redemption is already paid for, you will find the strength to face the darkest of days.

In a message prepared for the churches of Sri Lanka, and released just days after the tsunami disaster of Christmas 2004, Ajith Fernando points out that people of faith will often have a strength that they can share when they, and others, pass through a time of need

> Paul describes God as the 'God of all comfort, who comforts us in all our affliction, so that we may be able to comfort those who are in any affliction, with the comfort with which we ourselves are comforted by God' (2 Cor. 1:3-4). With so many people traumatised, sad and needing someone to listen to them, those who have received God's comfort can do much to be agents of healing. Even relief workers are in need of comfort today. What they have experienced is emotionally very draining. So Christians should be looking for opportunities to comfort people. Our role may often be simply being with and listening to hurting people. With the wounds so severe, people may not be in a position to listen to us. Like Jesus left heaven and came alongside us, we too may be called to leave our places of comfort in order to be close to our suffering people.[35]

Faith strengthens us and from that strength we are able to support and help others. The world cries out for people of such faith; people who can engage with the cultures in which they find themselves; who can make faith accessible and relevant but who also bring transformation to the world. Acoustic faith doesn't stop with listening; it takes listening further and becomes involved. It brings something to the party that makes a difference. This is faith that raises up the shapers of society; lovers of God who from their passion and presence will bring a new fragrance to the culture through which they walk. We listen because through listening we can learn. But faith calls us further. Beyond listening and learning, it calls us to love.

s t r e t c hing exercises

Love is listening

Consider the place of *listening* in your life. Have you always seen this as an important aspect of faith or is this a relatively new idea to you? Who is the 'best listener' that you know? What is it that they do, how does it impact those they meet and how might you grow in these same skills? In the area of evangelism and mission, how might an emphasis on *listening before answering* change the way your church relates to its community?

Take some time to pray. Talk to God about the issues that the concept of 'love as listening' has raised for you. Then create some space for silence. Listen to God in silence for a while. What is he saying to you about the role of listening in your life?

Resident aliens

Take some time to reflect on the phrase from the Lord's prayer 'Your kingdom come; your will be done, on earth as it is in Heaven'. If God's kingdom is coming to our world, what changes will it bring? Think of your immediate neighbourhood, of the UK as a whole and of the wider world. What do you see that the kingdom of God will drive away? What do you sense that the kingdom of God will bring?

Jot down some headline notes about your thoughts in this area, and make them the subject of prayer. Where do you feel challenged to engage more fully with the world in which you live? Where do you feel challenged to resist? Create some space for silence and ask God to bring to mind any specific areas in which he is trying to stretch your faith.

Transforming presence

Find Psalm 84 in whatever version of the Bible you think is most helpful – or in several if you have them. Take some time to meditate on verse 6, and on this image of pilgrims who have more impact on their circumstances than their circumstances have on them. Is this the kind of faith you have or long to have?

Ask God to show you the specific areas of your life in which you might pray towards bringing a 'transforming presence'. Are there people in need who might gain strength from the strength of your faith?

CHAPTER THREE

elastic

Shadrach, Meshach and Abednego replied to the king, 'O Nebuchadnezzar, we do not need to defend ourselves before you in this matter. If we are thrown into the blazing furnace, the God we serve is able to save us from it, and he will rescue us from your hand, O king. But even if he does not, we want you to know, O king, that we will not serve your gods or worship the image of gold you have set up' (Dan. 3:16-18).

elastic, *adj.* Having a tendency to recover the original form or size: springy: able to recover quickly a former state of condition after a shock (*fig.*): flexible: capable of stretching to include much... *Chambers Dictionary*[36]

elastic faith: faith that is stretched but not broken by the trials of life

An everyday super-mother

Helen Parr is an ordinary housewife, and a central character in one of the biggest box office successes of 2004. She has three children whose physical, emotional and educational needs, along with those of their insurance-industry father, take the full force of her gentle, loving, hard-working attention. But Helen Parr is no ordinary super-mother. Somewhere underneath her everyday, suburban skin, she is something else altogether: she is Elastigirl, a true superhero with spectacular powers. When the plot of *The Incredibles* demands it, loving mother and world-saving heroine combine into one and she lends her astounding flexibility to the complex task of saving her husband, the known world *and* her children. 'C'mon, ladies,' she says to camera. 'Leave saving the world to the men? I don't think so.' This is a mother who, when her children fall from a jet in mid flight, can form her body into a parachute and float them gently to the sea below; who can take the shape of a jet ski to find land; whose arms and legs can render enemies unconscious in four different rooms at the same time. This is a mother who is stretched but not broken by adversity.

What makes the character of Helen Parr so appealing in this animated *tour de force* is not the spectacular set-piece fights and rescues: it is that her spirit is as resilient and flexible as her body. Her faith in her husband, her love for her children, her commitment to help others and do good – these are the qualities that prove elastic enough to outwit, against the odds, a world-dominating super-villain. Of course she is just a cartoon character: a fictional creation who can be given any powers her author chooses for her. But unlike many cartoons, *The Incredibles* tries to show us the human side of its heroes and to paint a family with real weaknesses and concerns. It uses cartoon imagery to reflect back to us, perhaps, a little of the reality of our own, pressurised lives. And Helen Parr/Elastigirl is the true heroine of this hero-rich adventure. The energy that makes her so is the inner strength of love. The resilience demonstrated in Elastigirl's remarkable body is mirrored in Helen Parr's indomitable spirit.

Her spirit is as resilient and flexible as her body

This elasticity, this capacity to be stretched but not broken by the trials of life, is a mark of the faith in exile displayed by Daniel and, in Chapter 3 of his narrative, by Shadrach, Meshach and Abednego. God's promise to the Hebrew exiles, recorded in Isaiah 43:2,3, was that

> When you walk through the fire, you will not be burned; the flames will not set you ablaze. For I am the LORD, your God, the Holy One of Israel, your Saviour.

These general and metaphoric words become specific and real in the experience of Daniel's three young friends, as they face the very real flames of Nebuchadnezzar's furnace. Their response has been, for generations, a touchstone for believers who face the terror of opposition and even death.

The clear assertion of the narrative of Daniel, as the exile experience of all Israel is personified in the trials of a small group of young Hebrews, is that faith in Yahweh may not always bring deliverance *from* adversity but it will always bring deliverance *in* adversity. This is a graphic insight into the only kind of faith that will sustain us when the storms of life get beyond the teacup and actually start to frighten us. *Daniel and his friends are stretched across the enormous gulf between the affirmation that God can rescue them and the reality that he might not do so in the way they so desperately seek.* Their faith is not destroyed by adversity, because it is elastic enough to embrace this great gulf: the most significant gap in the human experience of faith.

Their faith is not destroyed by adversity

This is faith that only surfaces when the unthinkable happens; when God allows us to walk through a valley that is deeper, longer and darker than any we could imagine. It is the faith seen in the life of my friend Sue, who has walked with her dearly-loved son through the ravages of drug addiction and violent, paranoid schizophrenia. Sue has cried out to God time and again for his intervention; has seen things get worse not better; has heard from her own son tortured words that spring from a hatred whose origin she cannot begin to fathom: and yet she will not stop praying, or worshipping, or asking. Or believing. I have prayed with Sue on a number of occasions and wept with her, and I consider it a privilege to do so. For all that she endures, she carries in her heart a faith that I can hardly grasp. Above all, it is a faith that cannot be grounded in any expectation of comfort or ease: that cannot look to circumstance for its support. It is a faith forged deep within and shaped in the exile of a family plundered by the emotional burglary that is mental illness.

Daniel 3: The Fire Escape

Daniel Chapter 3 concerns the three young Hebrews named as Daniel's companions in Chapters 1 and 2. Promoted along with Daniel after his 'dream decoding' exploits, they have come to a place of prominence in Nebuchadnezzar's empire. But prominence brings its own complexities. There are rivalries amongst the civil servants of different faiths and the high profile given to the exiles draws stark attention to their distinction as Hebrews. They are pitted against the overwhelming power of Nebuchadnezzar himself, as he calls all his loyal servants to bow down to his image of gold.

In refusing to worship this statue, the three young Hebrews face the threat of death, which they meet with the remarkable words recorded in Daniel 3:16-18. Their faith is unshakeable – God can save them if he chooses, but if he chooses not to, he is still God. They will not bow. They are unharmed by the flames; a fourth figure is seen mysteriously alongside them, and the emperor must acknowledge the superiority of their God. He honours Shadrach, Meshach and Abednego, congratulates them for having defied his very command (v.28), ratifies the public worship of their God and promotes them again: this time not just because they are associates of Daniel but because they themselves have proved the power of God. Thus we are given one of Scripture's most memorable stories of faith under pressure – a story which has uplifted generations of God's followers.

> But when believers face some white-hot furnace they may be encouraged to be faithful to him, confident that their God is Lord of death and that he will demonstrate that he is. The power of paganism offers no ultimate threat. When

situations are utterly hopeless, they can trust him to vindicate their commitment and his power by rescuing them one way or the other.[37]

What is it that makes such a faith possible – that allows a believer to go on believing even when every fruit of belief is taken from them? When the thing you have most feared *happens*, when the stuff of nightmare is the stuff of everyday, how is it possible to honour the God who has promised to be with you?

Who's Who

Firstly, this 'elastic' faith is possible because our faith is rooted in *who God is*, not in who (or where) we are. Faith that is shaped and measured by circumstance, that takes its cue from the conditions in which we live, will prove itself, in the day of trial, no faith at all. The faith, by contrast, that will last is the faith that is anchored in the character and person of God. It is faith rooted not in the *believer* but in the *believed*.

> It is faith rooted not in the *believer* but in the *believed*

The Old Testament concept of faith as certainty and safety is deeply rooted in the Old Testament view of God. Faith fastens on God as One who by his nature is the sole certain and sure reality. God is faithful and unchanging, established in eternity; and because he is who he is, we can commit ourselves to him. ... the Old Testament views human response to God as vital in the matter of true faith. But the Old Testament emphasis (as expressed in the words chosen to express faith) is on this fact: our response to God has validity because God himself is utterly faithful and trustworthy.[38]

This is why it is significant that the people who can thrive in this kind of faith are not necessarily the same people who would thrive without it. They are not by definition positive people, who only needed some good techniques and psycho-babble to 'awaken the giant within'. They may even be the very opposite: weak, doubtful people who can't summon up the courage to challenge a milkman who overcharges them. But the difference is not in them – it is in God. It is not *their belief* that changes the world, it is *who they believe in*. It is faith in God, not faith in faith, that moves mountains.

The implication of this is that those whose faith will hold are those who know *who God is*. A second-hand familiarity with the supposed nature of God will not be enough nor will an academic acknowledgement of his attributes: only first-hand knowledge, like that a child has of a parent, will do and this is knowledge gained in the growing years of the everyday. It is the knowledge of God that I cultivate now – the relationship I invest in – that will deal with my fears when I am chilled by the cold winds of adversity.

Goodness Gracious Me

Secondly, elastic faith is rooted not so much in the *power* of God as in his *goodness*. It is because God can be trusted that I can leave with him the decision to rescue me or not. There is a significant aspect of the Hebrew notion of faith that is hidden in the different contemporary translations of Daniel 3:17. The NIV offers 'the God we serve is able to save us', as cited above. But the Good News Bible prefers the rendering 'If the God whom we serve is able to save us from the blazing furnace and from your power, then he will.' Other recent versions, including the New Revised Standard Version, agree with this translation, because it holds faithfully to an important theological truth about the Jewish faith. The exiles were committed to their God not primarily because of his *power* but because of his *goodness*. It is because God is *good* that he can ultimately be trusted in all circumstances and his goodness is not lost when circumstances seem to go against us.

The text of Daniel 3 is unafraid to acknowledge that Shadrach, Meshach and Abednego might simply *not know* whether Yahweh was powerful enough to save them. This ambivalence does not reduce their faith because what they do know – and on this their faith is founded – is that Yahweh will show them his goodness, that he can be trusted; that even in death they are safer with him than without him. Thus their faith runs no danger of drifting into mere positive thinking. They are not staring reality in the face and calling it unreality. They are not 'betting' their faith on a particular outcome. Rather they can say of their God, whatever the outcome, that 'he is good, and his love endures forever.' This is the foundational 'statement of faith' of the Old Testament period. God is good and his love can be trusted.

Perfect Parent

Thirdly, this liberates me to love God for his *person*, not for his *performance*. My prayers of faith are not instructions to a well-trained God, sending him coded signals to dictate his behaviour. I am not insisting that God must, at my command, perform the miracles I need. He is not a circus tiger, listening for my whistle. I am, rather, coming to a good and loving parent, who always wants the best for me and has told me that I must never be afraid, no matter how shamed, angry, confused or distressed I may be, to bring my needs to him. I come to him because to be at his side is to be secure; because to hear his voice and know his look is to be strong; because he is the first and only person in the universe whom I can trust to hear my cry and, without prejudice, to take me forward. In

> I come to him because to be at his side is to be secure

all this, the insistence that he *must* heal me in this particular way or provide for me in that, has no part in my conversation. He knows me. He loves me. How could I even think that this love, that sees to the very depths of my soul; this gaze before which no nuance is hidden; this light that caresses me and speaks me into being, could be manipulated into doing my bidding?

God is not a performing pony waiting for me to reward him with apples. He does not need to heal me in order to be God. He has already done enough for me to demonstrate his love: nothing more is necessary to prove it. I do not come to him to tell him *how* to save me. Rather, I throw myself on his mercy like a small boat trusting to the vastness of the sea, like a kite before the urging of the winds. I come to him because he is the source of all goodness: the only unpolluted fountain; the plumb-line of all that it true and pure and good. If he rescues me from the fire, so be it. If he asks me to walk through it, so be it. Either way, the story ends the same way: I fall into the bosom of his mercy.

Faith's New Song

Finally, elastic faith is wide enough and flexible enough to embrace the whole breadth of the experience of God; in the familiar and the unfamiliar, the easy and the hard. It faces the letters that bring bills as well as the letters that bring cheques. It responds to the night-time phone calls that tell of a death as well as those that rejoice in a new birth. It is there in the mornings that begin in birdsong and sunlight and usher in a day of apple-scented ease – and in the days that wake to clouds and traffic and bring hours of unbearable darkness. Elastic faith does not insist that circumstances adapt to us. It gives us the strength to adapt to our circumstances and rise above them.

Any British holiday-maker who has attempted to negotiate with a 'hole-in-the-ground' public toilet in France, Spain, Greece or North Africa will know how it feels for even the most trivial of things to be foreign to us. For the Hebrew exiles *everything* was foreign: they had to live out their faith in a new and sometimes hostile context. There were no maps for the journey God had sent them on. They were breaking new ground in the life and growth of Israel. And yet in their exile, they did find a 'way of faith'. Their achievement is remarkable and holds many lessons for us as we work out our own calling to faith in exile.

There is an important parallel between the experience of Shadrach, Meshach and Abednego and the question posed by the temple musicians in Psalm 137, in words immortalised in our own age by Boney M. Here the Jerusalem worship leaders mourn the loss of their land and role. Whatever their God has done, he has clearly not delivered them. They are passing through the very fire they have most feared. Their Babylonian tormentors call for them to sing the 'songs of Zion', but they can't bring themselves to do it. 'How can we sing the Lord's song in a strange land?'[39] they ask. So they stay silent and all too often we assume that this is the end of their story. But it is not. They go on to say

If I forget you, O Jerusalem,
  may my right hand forget its skill.
May my tongue cling to the roof of my mouth
  if I do not remember you,
if I do not consider Jerusalem
  my highest joy (Ps. 137:5,6).

What is the significance of these later verses? It is that these musicians have no intention of giving up their art. Our usual assumption is that in the face of oppression they have surrendered to silence, that they resolutely refuse to sing again. But if that were the case they wouldn't need to preserve their instrumental skills. It is not that they can no longer sing – their problem is that they have all the wrong songs. The songs they are being asked for are songs of joy and triumph: songs that celebrate Yahweh's victory over his enemies. They are psalms that remind Yahweh of his promise always to watch over Jerusalem; always to keep his people safe. The kinds of songs they had in mind might include passages such as

These musicians have no intention of giving up their art

God is our refuge and strength,
  an ever-present help in trouble.
Therefore we will not fear, though the earth give way
  and the mountains fall into the heart of the sea,
though its waters roar and foam
  and the mountains quake with their surging.
There is a river whose streams make glad the city of God,
  the holy place where the Most High dwells.
God is within her, she will not fall;
  God will help her at break of day.

Nations are in uproar, kingdoms fall;
  he lifts his voice, the earth melts.
The LORD Almighty is with us;
  the God of Jacob is our fortress.[40]

Think how it would sound to sing such songs before the
baying audience of the very captors who have ripped you
out of this safe reality? How hollow would these victory
chants appear? Would you feel, as you heard their jeering
laughter, that you were denying the integrity of the very
God you praised? How could you sing

He has set his foundation on the holy mountain;
  the LORD loves the gates of Zion
  more than all the dwellings of Jacob.
Glorious things are said of you,
O city of God:
'I will record Rahab and Babylon
  among those who acknowledge me –
Philistia too, and Tyre, along with Cush –
  and will say,'This one was born in Zion.'
Indeed, of Zion it will be said,
  'This one and that one were born in her,
and the Most High himself will establish her.'[41]

How can we sing songs of empty triumph, these musicians
are asking, when we are in a place of lament? How can we
celebrate false profits when our losses are so real? How can
we sing of God's promises when he appears to have broken
them? How can we sing of life in the face of such death? To
sing the songs of Jerusalem in Babylon is to devalue the
realities of God's leading: it is to live in denial rather than
faith. And Yahweh is not honoured in songs of denial.

What these musicians need is not silence: it is a different song. A song that acknowledges loss, yet looks to hope; that sees exile as a bend in the river but knows that the river will in due time reach the sea; a song that broadens the vision of God until he is big enough to rule not only over Jerusalem but over Babylon; not only through covenant-established

Not only in fair weather but in foul

Hebrew kings, but through pagan autocrats; not only in fair weather but in foul.

This is the song that Shadrach, Meshach and Abednego point towards when they declare that God is still God whether or not he delivers them from the fire. It is the song that Daniel, by his life, learns to sing; a song that embraces both the shadow and the light; that worships God in both testing and triumph. It is a song written not in the major key of exuberance but in the minor key of quiet confidence; a song that woos its enemies instead of going to war against them.

In the face of overwhelming decline, in a period of social transition that amounts to a kind of exile for the church, in this potentially post-Christian era, we don't need to stop singing; we need some new songs. We need a transition from singing out of our strength and abundance to singing out of our weakness and loss; from the blasting brass section of triumph to the soft solo harmonica of lament. Think of Sinead O'Connor, or Kiri Ti Kanawa; think of Jeff Buckley singing Leonard Cohen's *Alleluia*; think of Eva Cassidy or Norah Jones. Think of Leonard Bernstein and Stephen Sondheim's *There's A Place for Us* from *West Side Story*. Whatever your style of music, think of that perfect voice that takes the threads both of suffering and of joy, both of present pain and of future healing and weaves the realities both of loss and of promise into one, expressive song. Think of the depth of that song, of its beauty. Think of the real triumph that hovers underneath its melancholy chords. Think of the way in which its purity and passion *resonate* with your own heart and soul. And ask yourself – if that song was my faith, what would it look like?

One of the first Christians I met when I was converted at the age of thirteen was Eddy Tustian. Like most of those involved in the 'Jesus Movement' I had been drawn into, Eddy was a hippy who had spent much of his adult life to date moving from one squat to another, taking drugs and seeking out festivals, 'happenings' and esoteric experiences.

Long-haired and bearded, Eddy had endless stories to tell of his adventures on the hippy trail, from rolling a joint off-stage for Leonard Cohen at the Isle of Wight Festival to meeting Hayley Mills by a roadside in the home counties and being taken home for tea with John and the family. The stories were made more interesting by the fact that, unlike most of his hippy friends, Eddy was disabled from birth. He was confined to a wheelchair and travelled the country in one of the UK's distinctive 'invalid carriages', a pale blue fibreglass chariot-for-one for which Eddy held the all-time records for both speed attained and distance travelled.

One of the reasons he was such a great storyteller was

He embraced life with an energy that left many of us standing

that while others were out and about he had little choice but to sit for hours at a time, engaging in conversation with whoever was willing to sit with him. The Christian faith became for Eddy yet another great adventure and he plumbed its depths and scaled its heights with unbridled enthusiasm. From all the hours I spent with Eddy Tustian through my youth, often talking well into the early hours of the morning, the thing I most remember is his laughter. He embraced life with an energy that left many of us standing.

Part of Eddy's adventure of faith led him to be fascinated by, and involved in, a ministry of healing. He believed wholeheartedly that God answered prayer and was more than willing to pray for miracles, for himself and for others. Time after time, he saw prayer answered. And yet he himself never got up from his wheelchair. After I had left Bath, Eddy joined a large charismatic church in the city, where prayer for healing was a regular feature. Many services would end with an 'altar call' and those in need of prayer would be invited to the front of the meeting to receive it. Eddy delighted in telling me that at these times he would regularly wheel his chair to the very front of the room, where everyone could see him. It was a double act of faith. On the one hand, Eddy was saying to God that if healing was on offer, he could use it. Despite every disappointment, he would not allow the lack of healing to make him cynical: he kept his heart open to God's touch, however that touch came. But on the other hand, Eddy was also saying to the church 'I'm still here'. He was urging them, by his very visibility, to remember those who were not healed: to broaden their theology so that it could embrace not only the fact that God *could* heal but the evident reality that there were times when he did not.

I admire Eddy deeply for his act of double faith: for 'hanging in there' in a church that talked the talk of healing. All too often, these are the very churches that those in need most fear. Eddy learned to sing a song that is broad, rich and deep: a song that never lost the twinkle of the hope of healing, but never insisted, either, that God was not God unless he performed to order. What a delightful image of the true believer: that a man who has never in his life walked unaided should learn to dance so beautifully on the tightrope of faith.

This Grace

This grace we have been given is enough.

When the mountains set before us
Won't move by faith
Until by faith we start to climb.
It is enough.
When our cry for Heaven's miracles
Rings hollow, like a doorbell
Howling through an empty house.
It is enough.
When from our waiting-rooms of weakness
We say yes
To pressing on,
It is enough.
When we have reached the end of our energies,
And face the end of ourselves,
But can't yet see the end of our task,
It is enough
Enough
To know that you have loved us.
Enough.
That we are called before all time.
Enough.
That every fingerprint is valued.
Enough.
That you remember every name.
So we will embrace this grace.
And turn our hearts to face grace.

Loosening the locks
On our personal space,
We'll make each home a place of grace.
We'll drink from your wells
'til we're wasted on grace;
We'll speak out your words
'til our tongues taste of grace.
And we'll live to love your laws
Until our lives are laced with grace.
Down dark and dingy alleys
We will chase grace.
We will hold as something precious
every trace of grace.
We will celebrate and consecrate this grace,
because this grace we have been given,
is enough.

s t r e t c hing exercises

Stretched but not broken

Elastic; flexible; stretchable; resilient; adaptable; strong. Consider which of these words accurately describes your faith and character. Where they don't, what might it take for God to change you? What are the experiences in your life that have most stretched your faith? Were there occasions when God has clearly answered your prayers and you have grown as a result? Were there times when God has seemed not to answer at all? Did these also produce growth – or disappointment?

Reflect for a moment on your experience of 'elastic faith'. When your faith has been tested, has it stretched, or broken? What are the 'flashpoints' that most often push you to breaking point? As you reflect on these, ask God to show you ways, in his time, that you might deal with them. Pray for the gift of an elastic faith.

Faith's new song

Reflect on the difference between a faith that only looks for victory and triumph and a faith that embraces all the experiences God allows into our lives. How would it affect your prayer life and the worship of your church if you were to broaden your 'repertoire' to celebrate loss and deprivation as well as triumph? Would this be a new experience for you? What impact might it have on those around you?

Ask God to give you his 'full repertoire' of songs – to teach you to honour and worship at times of sadness as well as of joy; when you suffer loss as well as when you enjoy great victories.

This Grace

Take a few moments to read the poem *This Grace*. Read it a second time, and this time ask God to bring to mind, as you read, the particular areas in which it is relevant to you.

Take a few moments to pray for the grace of God to break anew into your life. Pray into each of the areas that have come to your mind as you have read the poem. Ask, in each area, that you would know the grace of God poured out on all those involved: and that you would know what it means, each day, that his grace is 'enough'.

CHAPTER FOUR

kenotic

'Therefore, O king, be pleased to accept my advice: Renounce your sins by doing what is right, and your wickedness by being kind to the oppressed. It may be that then your prosperity will continue' (Dan. 4:27).

kenotic, from **kenosis,** *n*. the self-limiting of the logos in incarnation…(Gr. Kenosis, emptying, from Phil. 2:7). *Chambers Dictionary*[42]

kenotic faith: faith expressed in servanthood and self-emptying

Giving back the Book

Like all such global figures, his Holiness the Pope is presented with gifts wherever he goes. Often these reflect the history and culture of the nation he is visiting or symbolise some special bond between that nation and the Roman Catholic Church. One such gift, given in the 1990s, carried a very different message.

The Pope was making a high-profile visit to Peru, where Catholic missionaries had built up, over many decades, a church of influence and power. To mark the occasion, a number of groups representing the indigenous peoples of the Andes worked together to write to his Holiness and to send an appropriate gift. Reflecting on the long and complex history of Christian mission in their region, in which the power of the cross had so often been allied to the power of the sword, they presented the Pope with the special gift of a Bible. In the letter that accompanied this gift, they said

> We peoples of the Andean countries of America decided to avail of your visit in order to give you back your Bible, because in five centuries it has brought neither love, nor peace, nor justice. Please take your Bible and give it back to our oppressors because they clearly need it moral precepts more than we do ...[43]

This was a highly imaginative action that captured in a simple gesture the disdain these people felt for a church that had come to them in the name of Christ and yet had brought so little Christlike love into their lives. Christians might well be offended by such gestures or rush to defend the record of their churches: but we should perhaps pause before adopting such a response. The record of the world's Christian churches is indeed bleak in its darker patches of oppression,

Christians might well be offended by such gestures

cruelty and violence. Even C. S. Lewis, a mild-mannered Oxford don known globally as a writer and theologian, was moved to capture this darker side of the church's history, insisting that someone, one day, would have to write a book that catalogued in openness and honesty the many ways in which Christians through history had contributed to the sum of human cruelty. Many in our world would not be free to hear our message, Lewis insisted, until they had seen us disown the terrible cruelties of our past.

This is the argument presented more recently by Australian urban missionary Dave Andrews. In his provocative book *Christi-Anarchy*,[44] Andrews claims that Christianity is so deeply linked to oppression and injustice, so indelibly marked by the violence of its past,

Christianity is so deeply linked to oppression and injustice

that it is time to start again with something new. Is it possible, Andrews asks, to stop worrying about whether people are *Christian* or not and help them, instead, to become more *Christlike*?

The thread that links C. S. Lewis, the indigenous peoples of the Andes and Dave Andrews is the recognition that, for all its glories, the church of Christ has committed terrible crimes in its twenty centuries of life and growth. For many commentators the issue at heart is of an *abuse of power*. It is when Christians take, hold and use power in ways that are not subjected to love that the image of Christ in the world is tainted. Alan Storkey, in a comprehensive assessment of *The Politics of Jesus*, makes this radical claim

> In the Gospels, we are presented with a perspective on power so radical and disturbing that few have understood or come to terms with it even today. For Jesus attacks the very notion of power as *control over*. Throughout human history, men have sought to control others, seeing that as the way to make their own lives more affluent, secure and free from work. Conquest, enslavement, control systems, state buttressing taxes, docile populations and manipulation have been normal parts of this cultural complex. Its costs are staggering.
>
> Human history is littered with castles, wars, slave trading, refugees, impoverishment, futile work, destruction, spy systems, bombing and other systems of effort which have resulted from the human need for *control over*. England loses its oaks to make battleships. Chechnya is flattened in a fight for control. Hitler devastates the lives of hundreds of millions in a need to dominate. Bombs are the most efficient way of wasting power ever invented. Although we may focus on the worst examples, the acceptance of *control over* is ordinary in the lives of many people and states. But what if this idiom is a great human mistake? This unthinkable truth Jesus has presented to us.[45]

Bombs are the most efficient way of wasting power ever invented

This same assessment of power and its uses is present in the book of Daniel. It runs as a thread through the narrative, continually calling into question the assumed omnipotence of the Babylonian kings. But it comes into sharp relief in Chapters 4 and 5.

Pride and prejudice

In two 'power encounters', separated by half a century, we see Daniel confronting two different rulers. There are subtle but significant differences in the ways in which the two rulers are portrayed. Nebuchadnezzar's treatment in the text is quite sympathetic. He is an all-powerful dictator and has crushed Israel but his character is not beyond redemption. In his later years, when God confronts his pride and he responds, he experiences a kind of conversion. At the end of his story, Nebuchadnezzar is presented as the king *repentant and restored*. By the end of Chapter 3 he has come to recognise the power of Daniel's God and to respect him but is still playing power games in his own life. By the end of Chapter 4 this is over, his recognition of Yahweh is complete and he is content simply to worship.

Belshazzar comes to the throne twenty-three years after the death of Nebuchadnezzar and is portrayed, by contrast, as a king *resistant and rejected*. A corrupt and immoral tyrant, he is presented in this narrative as beyond redemption.

> Belshazzar's first and final episode in the stories of Daniel is marked by his arrogance, blasphemy, idolatry.[46]

The king's decision to use the goblets taken from the Jerusalem temple – and kept safe for over sixty years in the treasure house of Babylon – is symbolic of both his disdain for Yahweh and his own depravity.

God's judgement on Belshazzar is swift and severe and the text wastes little time in sympathy for him: his defeat and death are recorded in less than half a sentence. Daniel has no need of his proffered riches and reward because he knows how fragile, in the context of God's sovereign power, the emperor's destiny is.

For all the differences between these two accounts and the characters of the kings central to them, the essential meaning of the stories is the same. Even though these men are amongst the most powerful figures on earth, even though in the world in which Daniel lives they have absolute power, yet still the sovereign God is more powerful. These stories present alternative views of the nature of true power

> On the one hand, the power of the king(s). This is a political power, imposed by military might, administered with unquestioned authority and maintained through fear. This is power as history tends to perceive it and as the majority of people accept it: the kind of power by which our lives are shaped and dominated.

> On the other hand, though, there is another power – the power that comes from knowing God. This is a more personal power, accessed through prayer, administered in weakness and maintained through trust in a sovereign God. This is a power rarely noticed by historians and unseen by many people but it is the kind of power by which history is truly made.

Through the confident faith by which he clings to the sovereignty of his God and the rich wisdom expressed in his life, Daniel is able to show that the power that comes from knowing God is ultimately stronger and more lasting than even the greatest political power. *Faith for Daniel is stretched between the evident and overwhelming power of the emperor and the apparent powerlessness of his own experience and situation.* But the experience of exile that begins, for Daniel, with the loss of power, ends in the discovery of a greater power still.

The loss of power, ends in the discovery of a greater power still

Turning the tide

The turning point of Nebuchadnezzar's story comes in Chapter 4, when Daniel presents to the king the two contrasting options for the use of his power, challenging him

> Therefore, O king, be pleased to accept my advice: Renounce your sins by doing what is right, and your wickedness by being kind to the oppressed. It may be that then your prosperity will continue (Dan. 4:27).

This, for Daniel, has been the purpose of God's dealings with Nebuchadnezzar: to convince the king that there is another way to live. Power can be used on behalf of the oppressed; authority and servanthood are not mutually exclusive.

Thus the hub of the book of Daniel is established; the central point around which so much of the action is arranged. Powerless, Daniel and the exiles have been brought by Babylon's superior force to live in captivity. Jerusalem is lost to them; their temple sacked; their God, it seems, defeated. The only reality now open to them is the dark reality of a pagan super-power, in which their Hebrew identity and faith has no currency. We wonder if they will be lost, crushed by the great beast that is Babylon, the majesty and memory of Yahweh erased with them. And yet the later chapters of Daniel reveal a confidence in God's future that is extraordinary. Daniel sees a coming kingdom, by which all the kingdoms of this

The only reality now open to them is the dark reality of a pagan super-power

world will be broken: a move of God that will subsume even Babylon. Stretched between these two extremes is Daniel's own journey through Babylon and at the heart of that journey is his stand before the kings.

In Nebuchadnezzar, Daniel is presented with the very embodiment of worldly power; the absolute monarch by whose whim whole nations are crushed, their gods discredited and mocked. And yet this king, confronted with the servant power of Yahweh's followers, is humbled. God reaches into his self-managed life and reduces him to worship. The reality of a sovereign God floors him and when he gets up off the floor he is a different man. Daniel is able to offer him, in simple words, the path of righteousness and mercy.

The heart of Daniel's story is a question of the true nature of power; his; the king's; God's. Only by embracing the true nature of power can Daniel or Nebuchadnezzar find their place in God's purposes and promise. The choice is stark: empire or obedience; present power or future promise; worldly might or the strength of an undivided spirit. The path of righteousness is the path of kindness to the oppressed. It is the way of mercy. The offer of God's power is an invitation to servanthood.

The crucial lesson to be learned here is that biblical faith is not about the abdication of power but about its right use. If all those who have a right sense of the sovereignty and love of God choose never to exercise power, in a global movement of pacifism and passivity, the unwanted result will be that only those who *covet* power will hold it. Some would claim, in contrast, that the best people to give power to are those who least want it. This is the theory behind the anarchic suggestion made in the USA some years ago that a new President should be chosen every four years not by campaigns resulting in a public vote, but by the random choice of an unsuspecting citizen: a kind of universal electoral lottery. Power, in this scenario, would always be given to someone who didn't seek it, rather than fought over by those who want it too much. The Bible seems to suggest that those who know how intoxicating and dangerous power can be should act redemptively not by avoiding power, but by exercising it well: using power on behalf of the powerless.

Any more empties?

In the New Testament, these questions of power and servanthood are given substance in the idea of *kenosis*, the self-emptying of Jesus. This is outlined in the words of Philippians 2:5-10, probably drawn from one of the hymns of the early church. Here it stands as the very essence of the ministry of Christ. *The Message* offers this translation

> Think of yourselves the way Christ Jesus thought of himself. He had equal status with God but didn't think so much of himself that he had to cling to the advantages of that status no matter what. Not at all. When the time

came, he set aside the privileges of deity and took on the status of a slave, became *human*! Having become human, he stayed human. It was an incredibly humbling process. He didn't claim special privileges. Instead, he lived a selfless, obedient life and then died a selfless, obedient death – and the worst kind of death at that: a crucifixion. Because of that obedience, God lifted him high and honoured him far beyond anyone or anything, ever, so that all created beings in heaven and on earth – even those long ago dead and buried – will bow in worship before this Jesus Christ and call out in praise that he is the Master of all, to the glorious honor of God the Father.[47]

The self-emptying of the cross undermines all earthly notions of authority, because Jesus does the very thing 'that kings cannot do and yet remain kings'[48] – he willingly surrenders his power. And yet this is his route to kingship. Jesus establishes once and for all that *to lead is to serve*.

Jesus establishes once and for all that *to lead is to serve*

My interest is 'kenosis' as a model of leadership was particularly aroused a number of years ago in France, when I met missionaries David and Diane Bjork. When I met the Bjorks they had been living and working in France for twenty years. They are American and had come to France to plant churches. That was what they were trained to do, and they set about it with skill and determination. But two years in something happened that rocked the Bjorks' world: they met a Catholic couple who seemed to have a faith every bit as deep and as real as their own. This was not part of their expectation, since they had assumed that the Catholic Church of France was a spent force with no capacity to bring contemporary people to faith. The new friendship brought David and Diane into contact with many other Catholics who were believers or seekers. Their church was not always an easy place in which to follow Christ in simple faith but it was the place they had chosen to do so.

Over a number of painful months, the Bjorks faced the crisis of deciding how they should respond to these new discoveries. Should they join their many Protestant friends in entirely rejecting the validity of the Catholic Church and preach openly against it? Or should they follow what seemed to be God's leading in supporting and helping those they now knew who were seeking to be evangelical followers of Jesus in the context of French Catholicism? God's promise to them on arriving in France had been that he would lead them on 'unfamiliar paths'[49] but they had never imagined that this would mean challenging the very basis on which they had been sent. In the end they made the choice to follow this strange new way and received permission from their sending agency to work as servant missionaries within the Catholic Church. Thus began an adventure that has continued to this day and has resulted in many French people coming to faith. There have been tensions and disappointments along the way. David and Diane Bjork have at times been ostracised by fellow missionaries: but they have also seen rich fruit in the lives of those God has called them to serve.

The importance of their story to me is the key role played by their understanding of mission as servanthood. During the crucial months in which they were deciding just how their missionary call to France would be played out, the idea of 'kenosis' became central to their thinking. If Jesus had fulfilled God's mission by emptying himself, setting aside his own rights and desires, might not God be calling them, also, to come 'empty-handed' into mission?

Might the very essence of missionary leadership be the call to set aside their own expectations and aspirations; their desire to create the kind of church that they were familiar with and instead to nurture a faith experience shaped by the aspirations of those they were called to serve? Fellow missionaries were quick to question the implications of the choice the Bjorks made, and to point to its perceived weaknesses as a missionary strategy. It would not lead, they insisted, to French people making a clear decision to become followers of Christ. It would not create new churches. There would be few, if any, measurable results. So much in this choice militated against the very basis on which the Bjorks, as Protestant missionaries, were sent to France. Yet it was a choice made because of a profound sense of a call to servant leadership, and I admire the Bjorks for the depth of their motivation. They set aside their own desires and plans in order to become the servants of others. In some small way, in the context of contemporary European mission, they caught hold of what self-emptying might mean.

Status, No

It is impossible to explore the biblical norms of leadership without encountering this central, recurring theme – the assertion that leaders are called to be servants. George Austin, Archdeacon of York, speaking of ordained leadership, has written that

> … the nature of priesthood carries with it a message for a wider society, that we were created for a purpose which may possibly not be centred on how much wealth we can amass, or on how successful we can be in climbing a ladder

> of ambition; that service to the community is a more
> valuable contribution than power and status. ... Servants,
> service, served: in speaking of the priesthood it is
> impossible to move far from these words.[50]

Picture the gloriously comic farmer boss of the film *Babe*.
Eschewing the spotlight for himself, he is deeply satisfied at
the applause offered to his remarkable sheep-pig. A slow
smile spreads across his guileless face as he mutters the
words of affirmation 'That'll do, Pig.' Servant leadership
invests in the cultivation of others and rejoices in their
achievements more highly than in its own.

The deeper our understanding of this organic
investment in the lives of others – our servanthood – the
more fully we will sever the unholy alliance of leadership
with status. Because leadership involves direction and
decisions; because it sets apart the leader from those they
lead, it all too often becomes tangled with notions of
position, platform and power. Even where leaders begin with
good intentions, they are easily
drawn into the misreading of their role as a statement of
personal worth. It takes courage, discernment, skill and
humility to fight this tendency and hold fast to a servant
calling. 'The Christian leaders who are truly to be trusted',
writes Ian Cowley in *Going Empty-Handed*, 'are those who
have come to know their own weakness.'[51]

Often we learn these lessons from those who think they
are learning from us. Kevin (not his real name) was a young
man Chrissie and I got to know when he was a teenager
and we were youth workers. He was linked to a church we
had some dealings with and became involved in the inter-

denominational youth ministry we helped to lead. Like many teenagers, Kevin dealt daily with anxiety and fear and the feeling that he didn't fit in and would never succeed in life. Unlike many others, he wasn't able to just brush this off as a passing phase. He found himself, at seventeen, drawn into a deep pit of panic and depression, until a series of crisis events led him to attempt suicide. He swallowed the best part of a bottle of sleeping pills and hacked at his wrist with a carving knife. Neither strategy proved fatal and Kevin ended up in the hospital rather than the morgue.

Kevin's 'cry for help' brought him into contact with a series of doctors and psychiatrists. It also led to the deepening of his Christian faith and, through the help and friendship of one of our youth workers, to a measure of healing. Just a few weeks after his suicide attempt, Kevin was with a group of us at a city-wide prayer event in Bristol. This was at a time when Romania was still a communist state and a cruel policy of 'systemisation' was forcing many peasants from their village homes into poorly-built concrete tower blocks. Christian photographer Jim Loring had been to Romania and had produced a moving series of slides on the crisis. We were urged to pray for the people of Romania, that this policy would be reversed and that change would come.

At the end of the meeting a few dozen young people went to the front to make a public commitment to pray and act for change. Kevin didn't join them. He was still too raw to make such a public display. But in his heart, he later told us, he made a simple commitment: to pray daily for these suffering people. His prayers continued for weeks and then months, as did

His prayers continued for weeks and then months

his healing. He finished his 'A' levels and went to university to study German. He spent a year on placement in Germany, still praying for the people of Romania. History, too, moved on, and great changes swept through communist Europe.

In time, Kevin was able to visit Romania, where he saw at first hand the ongoing suffering of its people. 'Systemisation' had been stopped, and the communist regime was gone but the country's notorious children's homes remained filled with unloved young people, without hope and without a future. Around four years after Kevin had made a promise to God that he would pray daily for the people of Romania, he moved there to work for one year as a volunteer in a children's home. He stayed for a second year and when the project he was part of ran out of time, he simply stayed in town. He rented a local flat, lived on the meagre income that was sent to him by a few friends in the UK and continued to love and support the young people he had met in the home, especially those who were now leaving and, without vocational guidance or help, were falling into the world of work or its absence.

In all, Kevin spent some four years in Romania, working largely in isolation and with virtually no resources. Throughout this time we received letters from him and I was deeply moved by his journey of faith. Here was a young man who had himself felt excluded by the strong and successful in his culture; who had lived on the margins. From his own experience of pain, he had grown to become a servant of others, living sacrificially through a period of life that for most of his peers was a time of carefree self-indulgence. He was courageous, committed and kind and he made a crucial difference to the lives of a small group of forgotten young people. He modelled servant faith and I admire him for it still.

Son of Man

When Jesus stands before Pilate, just as Daniel in his day confronted Nebuchadnezzar and Belshazzar, he speaks pointedly about the origins and workings of power. Pilate is the representative of Rome. His is the army that has crushed the Jewish state. He is the occupying force, the arbiter of life and death for all Israel. And yet Jesus insists that true power lies elsewhere.

> 'Do you refuse to speak to me?' Pilate said. 'Don't you realise I have power either to free you or to crucify you?' Jesus answered, 'You would have no power over me if it were not given to you from above. Therefore the one who handed me over to you is guilty of a greater sin.'[52]

This is a crucial moment in the revelation of Christ because it is here that the contrast is at its most stark between the might and power of Rome – politically derived, cruelly and militarily enforced – and the humble weakness of the Son of Man. The possibility that Jesus might have mobilised a popular army to drive the Romans out of Israel is not merely theoretical. It was a very real option in his time. Others had tried before him. Judas might well have wanted him to try again. He could so easily have rallied the people to fight force with force, to meet violence with violence, to win

The power of Jesus is not the power of force

freedom or die trying. But the power of Jesus is not the power of force: it is the power of self-giving. Only he knows, at this moment, that what he is doing is so much bigger than a Jewish revolution. He will give himself and in giving himself will prove that power need never again be

abused; that the violent do not win and that it is the meek
who will inherit God's creation.

The godly view of power, in this reading, is not given
only for leaders in the church. It is the standard against
which all leaders will be judged, whether they function in
religious, political, social or commercial fields. The Bible
reverses the polarity of power, surgically severing any
connection between power and status. If we have been
given resources, it is so that we might share them with
those who have nothing. If we are given power, it is so that
we might use it on behalf of the weak.

Breaking Babylon

The presence of this radical view of power in the book of
Daniel is highly significant as we seek a response to our
experience of exile. It tells us that *God's response to Babylon
is servanthood*. In the face of the military might and cultural
imperialism of this empire, God leads Daniel to respond
not in resistance and revenge but in faithful service. He is
not to stand against exile but to serve and worship God
within it. And in the end he has a greater influence on
Babylon this way than ever he would have as a commando.
There are important lessons here for all those caught up in
cycles of violence and repression: cycles that can only be
broken when someone takes the lead in forgiveness and
servanthood.

Kenotic faith calls us to re-evaluate our understanding of
power for two reasons.

- Because God is sovereign. Power does not belong to us
  but to God. Daniel's stance before Nebuchadnezzar is
  identical to that of Jesus before Pilate: he asserts that it is
  only *by God's permission* that any earthly ruler has power.

God is the true source of power and it is against his standards that we should judge ourselves. The image of Nebuchadnezzar as a tall tree in Daniel 4 resonates with the words of Ezekiel: 'I the LORD bring down the tall tree and make the low tree grow tall.'[53] No matter how much taller you are than those around you – or stronger, or more persuasive, or tougher – against the standards of the living God you are small indeed.

- Because leading is feeding. When a biblical understanding of power replaces *status* with *servanthood* as the heart of the equation, it challenges the fixation on control in our thinking. In place of control, *nurture* becomes the primary out-working of authority. Thus leaders are able to abandon an over-emphasis on control, because their goal is the growth and development of those they lead. At the very heart of our universe, at the point from which all things proceed, there is relationship. Nurture is the DNA of creation. Viv Thomas places servanthood at the very heart of leadership

In a world where many leaders are focussed on their own self-enhancement, projected image and drive to control, Jesus teaches us another way. It is a way of being powerful when you are weak, tough when you're soft and huge when you are small. It is absolutely subversive of the model given to us by a self-besotted world.[54]

However God calls us to serve him in the context of exile, he will call us to serve through self-giving. There is no other model for the task. To serve is to love and to love is to be empty of my expectations, my demands, my ambitions, so that I am free to live

To serve is to love and to love is to be empty of my expectations for others. The bold assertion of Daniel, as of Jesus, is that this is the path to true fulfilment. It is the seed that falls into the ground to die that ultimately finds life.

Healing Babylon

In our own Babylon, the exilic conditions of twenty-first century western culture, there will be key ways in which self-emptying and servanthood are the best possible response we can make to a culture in crisis.

As we face the apparent meltdown of Christendom, kenosis responds by urging us not to seek the rebuilding of the former power base of the church. We sense a cold wind blowing with the failing of the structures that have linked church and state, giving Christians privileged status, linking us to the majority power. Even those who have not experienced the direct marriage of church and state have benefited from it, with a history that has made Europe a 'friendly place' to be a Christian. But this is changing. We may be ridiculed by those who want a more open and fluid pluralism, we may find our views resisted, we may face criticism and even open hostility. The pluralism of post-modern culture tends towards pushing Christianity to the margins of the culture. But kenotic faith tells us that this can be a good and healthy place to be; that our faith has been powerless and marginal before and that it is from the margins that the story of Jesus has overturned empires. The place of weaknesses forces us into dependence on God's power and in dependence we reconnect with God's dream for our world. Kenosis urges us not to look back with nostalgia to the way things were before but rather to look forward to God's promise when every people group, including our own, will kneel before him. Do we have the courage to follow Jesus to the place of weakness, abandoning security to adventure with God on the margins?

As we struggle with the explosive growth of consumerism, kenosis tells us that self-love will never be the road to self-fulfilment. The unbridled pursuit of personal satisfaction; materially, emotionally, sexually and spiritually has become the mark of the market-driven culture that dominates more and more of our planet. This all-embracing philosophy, unspoken though it may be, is pervasive and hard to resist. Who will have the courage to say that another way is possible? Kenotic faith tells us that it is in living for others that we find life; that the road of obedience calls us to 'spend ourselves' for those who have nothing. As consumerism spreads its influence even to the former strongholds of Marxism, the bold and creative response of kenotic faith will increasingly stand out as the only sustainable response. Will we have the audacity to identify ourselves with the self-emptying of Jesus?

As we respond to the challenges of globalisation and multi-culturalism, kenosis tells us that it is possible to communicate across cultural divides without imperialism; that all cultures are worthy of our love and service; that no one culture bears God's exclusive imprint. Kenosis teaches us to value others; to set aside our own needs and ambitions; to love and serve all with equal passion. Where Christendom has created a monocultural vision of a God made in our own image, kenosis calls us to repentance and urges us to acts of loving service towards those we might once have excluded. In kenotic faith, my own culture is a costume I wear: I am not its prisoner. Dependent on God's power, I am not afraid to reach beyond my social comfort zones: to strip away the accretions of cosiness and conformity and meet my sister and brother soul to soul.

Are we ready to step out of the cultural castles we have built and embrace the image of Christ in friend and stranger?

Kenosis is frightening because the things we set aside are the very things that have given us security. We have a right to them. Jesus did not set aside his divine status because he was forced to but because he was willing to. He is the ultimate cosmic volunteer. He did not consider that he should 'grasp' his status, to protect it or to make sure he had an escape plan to fall back on. He launched himself on the purposes of God in history in total trust and surrender. How might the Babylons of our day be changed by a wave of such kenotic faith: by people who are not susceptible to the empty promises of power but choose, instead, to spend themselves for others? This is the spirit at the core of Christianity, the Unique Selling Point of a faith that is true to the ministry of Jesus. The way of Christ pits weaklings against emperors, shepherds against Goliaths. But they win, because they are armed with two world-changing weapons: trust and the willingness to live for others.

This is the spirit at the core of Christianity

The factor that makes kenosis so unattractive to some as an approach to mission and leadership it is that it simply doesn't measure up to objective strategic goals. Looking to the needs of others instead of looking out for number one takes us in a different direction to that suggested by many popular philosophies. So much of our consumer culture is based on the drive for self-fulfilment that self-emptying seems strange to us at best – and counter-productive at worse. Giving may be more satisfying than receiving, but it doesn't always seem more sensible. But kenosis is not a strategy; it is a value, an attitude, an approach. Once we

choose to adopt a kenotic faith, it will raise questions about our ambitions and dreams, our everyday attitudes, the way we decide who is important and who is not. Our values will fly in the face of so much received wisdom in the wider culture and, yes, in the church. It takes courage to pursue to its conclusion the assertion repeated by Jesus that the way to win is to lose; that the way to gain life is to give it – the spiritual equivalent of turkeys not only voting for Christmas but organising the hustings.

The Bible presents us with the strange and perhaps unique suggestion that it is in self-emptying that we will find the path to true self-fulfilment. Isaiah 58 suggests that personal and social renewal will come when we learn to 'spend ourselves' on behalf of others, especially those in great need.[55] Jesus repeatedly challenges his listeners to find their lives through losing them[56] and his own ministry is presented as that of a servant who gives himself for others.[57] Kenosis is a radical approach to life and it will call into question many of the assumptions of our culture, but it is an approach, it seems, that lies at the heart of the Christian gospel. Are we ready, in a post-Christendom age, to rediscover its power?

Poor amongst the poor

Kenotic faith not only calls us to act out of a place of weakness and poverty: it also calls us to stand with the poor and weak. To the extent that we ourselves are pushed to the margins of society, we become more able than ever to touch and bless the marginalised: not only the economically poor, but the lonely, the old, those given no viable place in our success-driven culture. The role of 'servant in society' so ably fulfilled by Daniel becomes, in the New Testament, the job description of the local church. Local churches come into being as 'colonies' of resident aliens, banding together for strength and security, living out their exilic destiny in cities that belong to others. These are communities of the weak amongst the weak, of the poor amongst the poor.

These are communities of the weak amongst the weak

The call to be 'poor amongst the poor' militates powerfully against a second mistaken reading of the New Testament concept of 'resident aliens' that has the potential to misguide the contemporary church. 'Gated communities' are a feature of the twenty-first century urban landscape in many parts of the world. The term is American, but the phenomenon exists in advanced cultures everywhere: a high-class housing development protected behind secure walls and railings and offering its residents a lifestyle cut off from the fears and failings of the society around them. Householders in these 'ghettoes for the rich' have all that they need, set apart from the horrors and hellishness of the city in which they are placed. Are there muggings on the streets of our city? Not here in our gated community. Has burglary become an urban epidemic? Not here in our gated community. Do strangers – criminals and drug dealers and desperate men among them – have free access to your streets and driveways, your corridors and service bays? Not here in our gated community. A gated community is a secure space in which those of privilege and wealth gather to protect themselves from the ravages of a world they can no longer control. It sells itself on fear and insecurity and its core trademark is exclusion: the social separation of sheep from goats. Are there too many goats messing up the herds in your streets? Join us now, in our sheep-only gated community.

This image is a universe away from the New Testament idea of 'resident aliens', but frighteningly close to the way that idea is often interpreted in our churches. It deals essentially in wealth, privilege, power and control: four attributes that are entirely absent from the New Testament term. Its goal is personal survival rather than the service of others. It is self-preserving rather than self-emptying. All too often it is the hidden code behind many of our church activities. Are our churches communities of the poor amongst the poor – or are they protectionist ghettoes offering a safe haven for the wealthy and privileged: the nearest spiritual equivalent to a 'gated community'?

The church behaves like a 'gated community' when it is more concerned with protecting and sustaining the lifestyle of its members than serving those in need in the community. When we are driven by fear to retreat from the culture and to hide behind walls of theological and social exclusivity, we become a gated community. When we grow congregations made up of just one social type – one colour, one background, one common lifestyle and do everything we can to defend our right to mingle like with like – we become a gated community. When we are blind to the very real poverty being experienced throughout the world by millions within the body of Christ as well as millions beyond it, and believe instead that our more comfortable lives are 'normal' – we become a gated community. Gated communities aim to keep the comfort inside and the problems outside and when the church does the same, it fails in its calling to kenosis.

The difference between a New Testament colony of 'resident aliens' and a twenty-first century 'gated community' is that the New Testament aliens generally couldn't afford gates. There were wealthy people amongst the early converts and influential politicians and business leaders did join but the tone of the first churches was set by their majority membership, drawn from the poorer classes. The resident aliens of the New Testament were not rich and powerful people protecting themselves from the ravages of the world – they were often themselves poor, resident only by the permission of a hostile power and aliens because they had no part in privilege and status.

The resident aliens of the New Testament were not rich and powerful people

Bamber Gascoigne, in his history of Christianity written to accompany a major TV series, notes that

[Jesus'] background was that of hard-working country people. Members of his own family are mentioned in Christian documents up to the third century. They seem to have remained fairly humble peasant farmers. And it was among such people that he found his disciples. … The early Christians in Rome … were almost all from the poorest classes, many of them slaves.[58]

South African missiologist David Bosch makes much the same observation

… the majority of Christians were simple folk with little education. The church was not a bearer of culture. As a matter of fact, it was held in contempt by the vast majority of the cultured citizens of the Empire.[59]

More recently John Holdsworth has explored the social implications of the term 'resident aliens'

Research into the socio-political context of first-century Asia Minor suggests that the Greek term *paroika* has a technical sense of 'resident aliens' akin to asylum-seekers perhaps in Britain or, more precisely, Turkish guest-workers in Germany. They have permission to be where they are but they are not citizens and there is nothing permanent or guaranteed about their continuing there.[60]

The significance of these different voices is that they together put to death the notion of the early church as a community of privilege and power. The churches of Christianity's first few centuries were predominantly communities of the poor amongst the poor. The notion of the church as an island of privilege is a more recent historical development but one that has become, for many people, the dominant image.

Perhaps a more accurate metaphor for the New Testament concept of 'resident aliens' would be that of a shanty town or refugee camp. Here the exiles of the earth are pressed together, here the poor and the desperate seek shelter, here you must live shoulder-to-shoulder with the destitute. Or picture a London air-raid shelter at the height of the Blitz; open to all; crowded, chaotic, with cups of strong, sweet tea for all who need them. In the biblical vision of an alien colony, the church does not *choose* whether to have a ministry among the poor because it is immovably established among the poor. It is set in the very streets in which the muggings happen, where the poor struggle for survival and crime and corruption are rife. A Bible-study group firmly planted in the festering streets of a slum development is

> **Picture a London air-raid shelter at the height of the Blitz**

perhaps the closest we can get to the New Testament image of resident aliens. The concept is not an escape clause. It does not call us, for fear of the world, to create Christian ghettoes. It calls us, rather, to immerse ourselves amongst the dispossessed, to find fellowship with others who, like us, are refused the power and privilege of Babylon: to see the kingdom come amongst the last, the lost and the least.

Such a model does not exclude the rich and privileged from the church nor does it preclude the planting of churches in rich neighbourhoods. But it does insist that the essence of the gospel is inclusion; that wherever the church is *located* it should be *orientated* towards serving the poor. Kenosis is not a place we stand, it is a direction we face and it shapes our every ambition and aspiration.

When Nicola and Sandra Skrinaric heard God's call to pastor a church in Mostar, Bosnia, at the height of the war, they took on a community under siege. The converted TV repair shop that served as a gathering place for the young church was right in the line of opposing snipers. For a time it was impossible to enter or leave the building without running in an exaggerated switchback line, zig-zagging through the possibility of instant death. But people came and the church grew because it was there where it was needed. There was danger, loss and pain for those who led the church but to those in the city for whom danger, loss and pain were daily companions, this was a miracle of hope. Why does it take a war to bring out in God's people this courage, this willingness to serve and suffer?

How to get blessed by the Father

I have often been challenged by Jesus' words in Chapter 25 of Matthew's gospel, describing the future day when God will separate 'the sheep from the goats'. To the sheep, whom Jesus describes as 'blessed by my father' he says

> I was hungry and you gave me something to eat, I was thirsty and you gave me something to drink, I was a stranger and you invited me in, I needed clothes and you clothed me, I was sick and you looked after me, I was in prison and you came to visit me.[61]

But interestingly the sheep in Jesus' narrative do not respond by thanking God for his affirmation. Rather they say, 'When did we do this?' Like many of the questions in Scripture, the very strangeness of this response should push us to probe further. Why do the 'sheep' ask this question? The implication of the text is that they ask because they can't remember doing these things to Jesus. They can't remember caring for the sick Jesus. They can't remember visiting Jesus as a prisoner. They can't remember helping the hungry and thirsty Jesus and welcoming Jesus the stranger. They can't even remember clothing the naked Jesus. A naked, hungry Jesus just released from prison has burst into the middle of their Bible study – *and they can't remember?* There are only three possible explanations for this response and its impact on the picture Jesus is painting:

- They never did these things, and it is God who has got his history wrong.
- They did these things, but are suffering from a unique and bizarre case of corporate amnesia – presumably a condition that particularly affects sheep.
- They did these things so often, and so naturally, so much as a part of their everyday lives, that they never even noticed that Jesus was involved.

The third of these is the option suggested by the text. These people are commended not only for doing good, but for doing good without even realising it. How does this happen? How does such a natural facility for the poor and the weak, such a comfort around strangers, such an ease with helping others become the mark of our lives? Part of the answer is that this is what happens to us when these are the people we naturally hang out with. As Jesus commends these selfless sheep, they are running through their memory banks, urgently assessing the information they have been given. So *which* prisoner was it, of the many, that was Jesus? Of all the sick we tended, of all the hungry we fed, of all the naked we clothed, *which was Jesus?*

The answer, of course, is that they all were, as Mother Teresa has so movingly reminded the world. But the point of the story is this: if the hungry and thirsty, the sick and naked, the stranger and the prisoner *are the people you hang out with*, helping them

The poor will not be a programme your church has proudly advertised

and blessing them and standing with them in their exile will be a natural part of your life. The poor will not be a programme your church has proudly advertised. They will be your friends. How do you make a despised Samaritan your neighbour? Travel from Jerusalem to Jericho. How do you make of exiles your friends? Let God throw you from Jerusalem to Babylon. Sing the Lord's song where the Lord's song needs singing. Be exiled among exiles, be weak amongst the powerless, be poor in the midst of the poor.

I recently met a Christian woman whose life had not long ago taken several turns for the worse. Her marriage had failed and she had faced a desperate journey through alcoholism and a series of related addictions. She had been wealthy and from a 'good' social background but such were her troubles that she had eventually spent time living on the street. By the time we met, she had begun to piece her life back together and was once more housed, working, sober and solvent. Her experiences had nonetheless marked her. One of the fruits of her journey was that many of the people she had formerly thought of as social victims were now her peers. 'These are not just people I know', she said, speaking of the tramps and lap dancers, the dealers and prostitutes who at her lowest point had come into her life, 'they are my friends.'

I was deeply moved to hear this articulate, educated woman speak with such frankness. I believe she was expressing the only true basis on which the church *can* work amongst the poor. Unusual though her journey was, she had stumbled across one of the deepest truths of the gospel: we cannot serve our neighbour until our neighbour is our friend.

The purpose of a gated community is to keep these very people out: the hungry, the thirsty, the stranger, the naked, the sick, the prisoners. If a naked, hungry stranger, just released from prison, strays onto the avenues of a gated community, how long will it be before the police arrive? If a naked, hungry stranger, just released from prison strays into the aisles of your *church*, how long will it be before the deacons come? Perhaps these are the lessons that we learn, as communities of Christ's followers, when we pass through times that we experience as exile.

I am challenged by these words even as I write them because my life, like the lives of so many in the church today, is lived in the comforting glow of a middle-class home and income. I try to buy a copy of the *Big Issue* whenever one is offered to me but I am a customer to those who sell them, not a friend. I buy fairly-traded coffee but only at the same time as a trolley full of other delights and delicacies: few of which have been traded in a manner that is even remotely fair. I classify the poor as victims of poverty; targets of charity, there to be helped. I rarely classify them as equals. I rarely view the world from their perspective. But I suspect I am the poorer for it. I suspect, and some of the moments when God has brought revelation into my life through loss stand as

I classify the poor as victims of poverty

evidence for this, that my vision of the kingdom would be that much stronger if I viewed it more often from the standpoint of the poor. In this light, hard as I might find it, I *welcome* God's efforts to thrust me into exile. In whatever small ways I can, I want to embrace life as seen from the underbelly of misfortune. Might this mean spending some time with the person whose needs are a challenge and an embarrassment to me – instead of moving quickly on? Might it mean harnessing my talents and energies and, yes, my income, to use it on behalf of those in need? Might it mean praying more; doing more; caring more for those who are losers in the current global wave of consumerism?

This is a difficult journey, and one on which others have made more progress than I have: but it is one I believe we must make, as Christ's body in Babylon. In the thirty or more years that I have been a member of the evangelical community in the UK, I have seen that community become richer, more comfortable and more unquestioningly middle-class than ever it was in its roots. 'Trickle-down' prosperity in western culture has raised the living standards of many Christians in significant ways. But in the same period the plight faced by the world's poor has grown more desperate. Is there a grave danger that our churches will be islands of privilege amongst the privileged, gatherings of power amongst the powerful? Are we creating spiritual gated communities? If we are, then it will be our experiences of exile that most help us: thrusting us from privilege to poverty; from freedom to fragility. It is when we are taken from having-it-all to going empty-handed that we most learn the power of the gospel. Perhaps exile, far from being a curse on our lives, is our salvation. Perhaps exile is God's gift to the western church.

When my good friend Lowell Sheppard was the Director of British Youth for Christ, he and his wife Kande had their first child, Luke. Luke's birth was complicated and he only lived for a few hours. In a single day Lowell and Kande were taken from the heights of joy at their first experience of parenthood to the very depths of despair at such a terrible bereavement. I often worked and travelled with Lowell in the months following this tragedy and regularly heard him preach. He spoke of the darkness of the days following his young son's death and of the comfort that had come to him from a particular passage of Scripture. It was a psalm that spoke of being 'hidden under the shadow of God's wing.'[62]

The desperation of bereavement had been, for Lowell and Kande, a discovery of the 'shadow side' of following Christ. As long-term believers, they had a faith that sustained them through these days but in that faith they discovered that even in God's tender care, there are dark days. Lowell spoke movingly of how this brought home to him the reality of faith and the truth that it is not until you have seen life 'from its underbelly' that you truly know what faith is. He remembered singing as a child the negro spirituals written on the slave fields of America but it wasn't until he faced his own great lost that he grasped the depth of these redemption songs. Luke's death was a loss that

Lowell and Kande would never want to live through again
– and who would ever ask that they should? But it was not
a loss from which they failed to learn. It brought fruit in
their lives because it showed them how different faith is
when it is seen from the place of loss and pain.

God calls us, I believe, to be poor amongst the poor
because that is the viewpoint from which the world most
makes sense. When I studied art at school, a favourite trick of
my teacher's was to take a half-completed drawing and turn
it upside down. They knew that most drawings, to the eyes of
the would-be artist, look like the thing drawn. Just as would-
be pianists will often 'hear' a
tune they have picked out on
the piano even though no one
else in the room hears
anything but discord, a
combination of wishful
thinking, projection and self-
deception makes it hard for students to see whether their
drawing is any good. But turn the page upside down and
the spell is broken. The clues are lost and it is only if the
perspective and shading are right, if the drawing has been
skilful, that a meaningful shape will be discerned. Seeing the
world from the perspective of the poor is the equivalent of
turning the drawing upside down. It can provide a reality
check on our faith, a test of whether what we are creating
really has substance. For individuals, families and local
churches and for the church as a body dispersed across a
culture, there is a lot to be gained from asking from time to
time the question: 'What impact are our actions having on
the poorest of the poor?'

> **God calls us, I believe, to be poor amongst the poor**

s t r e t c hing exercises

Power

How do the contrasting images of power – Daniel versus Nebuchadnezzar; Jesus versus Pilate – affect the way you think about life and mission? Are there key ways in which a gospel that turns on its head the more usual understanding of power might change the way you operate as a Christian?

Find time and space to think and ask God to bring to mind any areas in which you have tended to abuse or hold on to power. Don't go looking for a guilt-trip but remain open to God's genuine conviction. In your marriage and home, in your professional relationships, in your church and community, are there times when you have been more like Nebuchadnezzar than Daniel; more like Pilate than Jesus? Ask God to lead you through repentance into healing and to give you a righteous and constructive approach to the exercising of power.

Self-emptying

What issues does the idea of 'kenosis' (self-emptying) raise in your life? Where might God be asking you to lay aside your own rights and privileges in order to serve others? Is this something you feel you can do or are the costs and implications too enormous to consider?

Seek God for a clear way forward. If it will take time to adopt a more servant-like approach, set yourself some targets. If you don't know of any area in which this challenge to servanthood is real for you, rejoice in this and ask God to give you the name of a person, a family or a people group whom you can commit to serve. Commit to creating a little holy chaos in the world by perpetrating 'random acts of kindness' in your church and community.

Poor amongst the poor

Does the vision of the church as a shanty town or refugee camp fill you with horror or with excitement? How and where might God be calling you to be 'poor amongst the poor'? What first steps can you take towards this calling?

Throughout Scripture, God is seen to have a heart for the poor. Take some time to examine your own heart and to ask how God might lead you into a greater awareness of the poor in our world and a greater engagement with and alongside them. What might it mean for you to follow the advice of Bob Pierce, founder of World Vision, to 'find out what breaks the heart of God, and pray that it will break yours too'? As you reflect on the church, on the poor and on the needs of the world, what names and faces does God bring to your mind?

CHAPTER FIVE

poetic

Then Daniel answered the king, 'You may keep your gifts for yourself and give your rewards to someone else. Nevertheless, I will read the writing for the king and tell him what it means (Dan. 5:17).

poetic, from **poem,** *n.* a composition in verse: a composition of high beauty of thought or language and artistic form typically, but not necessarily, in verse: anything supremely harmonious and satisfying... *Chambers Dictionary*[63]

poetic faith: faith that opens the imagination to God's beauty

A sword seen in the streets of Bath

Everyone remembers a favourite teacher: not necessarily the one they most liked, but the one who most inspired them, who had most impact on their life. More often than not, the person they remember is the person who most openly believed in them. I have two and both, in their way, were poets.

The first was a poet by training and choice. David Grubb was my class tutor and English teacher for my first three years of senior school. He was a published poet and did everything he could to nudge us in the same direction. Under his leadership we started a new school magazine, *Mad Dog*, named from a line in Sheridan's *The Rivals*: 'A sword seen in the streets of Bath would raise such an alarm as a mad dog'. We entered local poetry competitions and the few of us who showed an aptitude for poetry were taken to readings in the area, where both he and we would perform. This was an adult world and a specialist one at that, and the impact of exposure to it stayed with me. Years later when writing and performing poetry became an important part of my life, I was grateful for those formative experiences.

This was an adult world and a specialist one at that

My second great teacher was not in any literal sense a poet but he showed me more than anyone I knew what a poetic life might look like. Peter Coard was my 'A' level art teacher. Anti-establishment and often cantankerous, he was a brilliant artist, a passionate student of the history of art and architecture and an inspiring and demanding teacher. He was a master of pen and ink drawing and as he taught us he would demonstrate through sketches and scribbles that left us breathless.

But more than anything, he inspired me by what he did outside school hours.

We lived in the city of Bath, one of Britain's most exceptional architectural treasure-stores. On almost every street, from the cramped terraces of Victorian workers' cottages to the curved splendour of the Georgian crescents, there were architectural features of rare value and arresting beauty. But this was the 1970s, an era of thoughtless modernisation and heartless redevelopment. Every month another classic building, or a whole street, or a redundant early-industrial neighbourhood would be flattened. 'Farewell to old Bath, we who knew you are sorry' wrote the poet Laureate John Betjeman. 'They've carted you off in a developer's lorry.'

Peter Coard was schooled enough in the history of architecture to know that some of the features that were falling to the wrecking crews existed nowhere else in the world, and would never be seen again. He wasn't prepared to see such treasures lost without a fight so he fought back with the

He wasn't prepared to see such treasures lost without a fight

only weapons he knew: pen and paper. When a new site was scheduled for demolition, he would step in ahead of the work crews and, racing against the ticking clock, would sketch the features so soon to be destroyed: here a Georgian boot-scraper; there a window moulding. Roof slates; chimney pots; door frames; porches and porticoes: the tiniest of details would be lovingly and meticulously captured and against each a note of the exact time and location of the drawing. Like a botanist of the urban jungle, seeking out species on the verge of extinction, he turned his eye for detail and his skill in reproducing it into a loving act of public service.

The result was a series of three volumes called *Vanishing Bath*,[64] in which the pages of Peter's notebooks were beautifully recreated. Though passionate, Peter Coard was not a cheerful man. He made little effort to hide the anger he felt at such destruction. When he discovered that I lived with my family in a block of council flats whose construction had necessitated the demolition of five whole streets of terraced cottages, he let me know in no uncertain terms how much he disapproved. I was never quite forgiven for my address. Neither was he sympathetic to my faith. But there was something redemptive and beautiful in his response. He would work late into the failing light of evening, sometimes drawing just minutes before the walls came down. He was a prophet of pen and ink, a subversive with a sketchpad. There was a passion in his work that no utilitarian analysis could match. I later found out what most of us didn't know at the time – that his eyesight was also slowly failing. The clock was ticking in more ways than one.

I'm not sure if *Vanishing Bath* is still in print, or if history will hold a place of honour for Peter Coard. But I do know that his example will always live with me. David Grubb introduced me to the specific art of poetry but it was Peter Coard, I believe, who showed me how to use it. He was a picture of a life lived poetically.

Poets in a world of prose

Poetry, in this sense, is not simply a way of writing. It is not about rhyme and rhythm, or about setting out words in verse form. It is about seeing imaginatively; about acting intuitively; about valuing beauty; about living in artful openness. In the realm of faith, a poetic stance will not allow the truth and beauty of God to be reduced to bald statements and cold logic. It embraces mystery; it lives with metaphor, it looks always towards a bigger picture. This sense of *living poetically* has been central, for many years, to the work of Old Testament scholar Walter Brueggemann

> To address the issue of a truth greatly reduced requires us to be *poets that speak against a prose world*. The terms of that phrase are readily misunderstood. By prose I refer to a world that is organised in settled formulae, so that even pastoral prayers and love letters sound like memos. By poetry, I do not mean rhyme, rhythm, or meter, but language that moves like Bob Gibson's fast ball, that jumps at the right moment, that breaks open old worlds with surprise, abrasion and pace.[65]

Brian McClaren, who has written extensively in the American context of the challenges facing the church in post-modern culture, suggests that the recovery of poetry is one of the most urgent needs facing the church of our age, as we interact with a world that has forgotten that God is beautiful.

> Our words will seek to be servants of mystery, not removers of it as they were in the old world. They will convey a message that is clear yet mysterious, simple yet mysterious, substantial yet mysterious. My faith developed in the old

Our words will seek to be servants of mystery

world of many words, in a naïve confidence in the power of many words, as if the mysteries of faith could be captured like fine-print conditions in a legal document and reduced to safe equations. Mysteries, however, cannot be captured so precisely. Freeze-dried coffee, butterflies on pins and frogs in formaldehyde all lose something in our attempts at capturing, defining, preserving and rendering them less jumpy, flighty or fluid. In the new world, we will understand this a little better.[66]

This poetic faith is present in the life and ministry of Daniel in significant measure. It shapes the ways in which he communicates with the succession of kings he is called to serve, as dreams and visions are expressed in metaphor and enigma. In Chapter 5 this gift takes centre stage, when Daniel is called in to interpret 'the writing on the wall'. We have already briefly considered this chapter, alongside Chapter 4, in its implications for our understanding of power. But it is also important for what it has to say to us about poetry. *Daniel is stretched across the imaginative chasm between the immeasurable depths of God's mystery and its concrete expression in words and images*. His response to this chasm is, in part, to adopt a poetic approach to faith and its communication. As such, he has much to say to our own age, in which the message of God to our culture has all too often been reduced to an uninspiring formula.

Why is it that evangelical Christians, marked out as they are by their supposed commitment to evangelism, are so earth-shatteringly bad at sharing their faith? Why is it that for all the cajoling and guilt-inducement that goes on, for all the training courses and schemes, for all the aids and resources offered, that most Christians find it extraordinarily hard to talk about their faith among those who do not share it? Why do you work in an office where hardly anyone even knows that you are a Christian? Why did I have to own up to the fact, leaving a house I had lived in for four years, that I hadn't in all that time had a meaningful conversation with even one of my neighbours?

And yet we can talk about football and TV and the terrible plight of coastal Asia devastated by the world's worst tsunami. We can show off our new car down to the tiniest detail of its micro-chip managed wizardry. We can compare our various children's achievements and hold forth eloquently on where we shop and why and which is our favourite brand of trainers. Part of the answer to these important questions is that there is a gap between faith and imagination in our own lives. We ourselves are neither inspired nor stirred by faith, much as we think we 'ought' to be. There are places in our lives where our senses are stirred, where imagination is ignited, where simple, human enthusiasm takes flight. And there are places where faith is found – but the two all too rarely meet. Do we need, like Daniel, to discover the clarity with which God speaks in the places where the spark of creativity glows brightest?

It could be you

Daniel is called upon because Belshazzar, at the height of a drunken feast, is terrified by a disembodied hand that has etched a message on his dining-room wall. None of the wise men of Babylon can understand God's graffiti. Only Daniel is able to interpret it.

It is impossible to say exactly how the words or letters that appeared on the wall were set out, but it is significant that the wise men can neither read *nor* interpret the script. Al Wolters has recently suggested that they may have stumbled because what they saw was a series of unbroken letters (*scripta continua*) with no indication as to how they should be divided. Daniel's interpretation divides this 'code' into three words of three letters each, each of which has three levels of meaning, depending on the exact pronunciation chosen. The final of these three levels of meaning, Wolters argues, sets out the consequences of God's judgement on Babylon: 'He has paid out, you are too light, Persia!' All three levels of meaning suggest a theme of scales and weights, made more significant when we know that this event took place on the exact day of the annual rising of Libra in Babylon's astrological system.[67]

The importance of this interpretation is that it brings out the poetic nature of this communication. God's message operates at several levels; it resonates with the Babylonian religious system and it arrests the king's attention with mystery and metaphor. God speaks in riddles to us, not so that we won't understand but so that we will be drawn in to the search for a deeper understanding. As the interpretation is brought, explosions would be taking place in the mind of the king, layers of meaning tumbling over him and triggering a deep realisation of God's judgement. The message is sharp, decisive and perfectly aimed and it hits its target right between the eyes.

God's message operates at several levels

Had Daniel been asked to take to the king the message of God's judgement in blunt, direct form, it is unlikely that he would have gained an audience. It is the intriguing event of a hand writing on the wall and the mysterious nature of that which was written, that grips the king's imagination. This parallels the ministries of prophets throughout the Old Testament. The prophets are encouraged by Yahweh to proclaim their prophecies in rich imaginative language and often in beautiful poetic form. They are called to set up stunts and object-lessons to catch the attention of kings, rulers and people. The book of Isaiah qualifies both as prophecy and as poetry: Ezekiel is a conceptual artist worthy of the Tate Modern. Prophecy, in the Old Testament context, is playful, colourful and meaningful: it is communication that hangs suspended between art and mission. There are wordplays to drive home the warnings God is bringing, there are passages of lament that cut to the heart with their mournful beauty. There are images, not least of God himself in his care for his people, that sink more deeply into the mind and spirit than mere instructions ever could. Poetry speaks to the whole person, with messages that sometimes bypass the sentry-points of rationality, delivering their punch straight to the heart and will.

Poetic proclamation

The embracing of a poetic faith will deeply change the ways in which we engage with our culture, bringing renewal to the whole area of mission and evangelism. In our time this may well prove one of the central challenges facing the western church. A proclamation that relies on the simple transmission of a series of facts or propositions will not capture the post-modern imagination. Perhaps in the era of modern certainties it had its place but no more. The twenty-first century is more similar in this sense to the first than to the twentieth. An appreciation of mystery has returned to our thinking and expectations.

Take, for example, the central message of the gospel announcement, the willingness of God incarnate to die a criminal's death. The cross is almost certainly the most intriguing symbol at the heart of our culture as Europeans. We are drawn to it, even if we don't all profess allegiance to it. It is an unfathomable mystery, before which we can only gaze in wonder, as did the thousands who filed through the National Gallery in London to visit the 2001 'Seeing Salvation' exhibition. Jack Miles notes in his controversial book *Christ: A Crisis in the Life of God* that the crucifixion of God is the deepest mystery in our 'cultural DNA', 'the primal scene of Western religion and Western art.'[68] Unlike art and poetry, evangelism has tended towards the belief that great mysteries can be reduced to simple terms: that all can be explained. I believe this approach is failing and will continue to do so. Far from asking for the mysteries of life to be explained to them, contemporary seekers believe that only mystery can be trusted. A God who can be easily explained in a series of short propositions is no God worth knowing.

I believe this approach is failing and will continue to do so

It is an unexpected development, but it now seems that some of our explanations of the gospel may be more of a hindrance than a help to those seeking faith. Many of those who are rejecting our formulaic explanations and reductions are very willing to stand in silence before the mystery of a God prepared to die. This is not a mystery that they sense they are *meant* to fully understand. Rather it is a mystery into whose depths and richness they can but gaze in wonder. Do we need to replace the invitation to 'come and hear it all explained' with an invitation to 'come and wonder at the mystery'? This is not to suggest that we should never explore the theological realities wrapped up in the life and death of Jesus, nor that we are never meant to know what happened and why: it is rather to suggest that our 'knowing' is meant to carry both poetry *and* logic. All knowledge of God should move us to worship and worship is a poetic, creative, mysterious activity.

Paul seems to understand this instinctively with his Athenian audience.[69] He incorporates poetry into his speech and is unafraid to present paradox. He speaks of God as the One in whom 'we live and move and have our being' – the mysterious force at the heart of the universe. He establishes the paradox whereby God is both known and unknown, both familiar and strange. The God of Paul's gospel is already as close as breath to these pagans and yet at the same time is a new and unknown force to be reckoned with.

It is important to note, in this embracing of the depths of mystery in communication, that Scripture presents an intriguing paradox. Mystery, in the Bible, is used not to hide truth but to reveal it. Poetry in Scripture expresses and communicates, making truth known. The creativity of Jesus serves to reveal and uncover. When Jesus taught in parables, he clearly did so in order that the truths might sink even deeper into the minds and hearts of those who listened. So compelling was this communication style that Matthew's gospel breaks into a particularly poetic narrative to remark that Jesus fulfils perfectly the prophecy of Psalm 78: 'I will open my mouth in parables, I will utter things hidden since the creation of the world.'[70] This contrasts starkly with the all-too-prevalent pattern of the post-modern age, where the concept of mystery is used to mask and deny; to hide the very possibility of truth under a cloud of confusion and distortion. Our calling as Christians is to be creative, imaginative and poetic in order to communicate truth, not to mask it. Scripture affirms that in Christ, the mystery of God has been revealed in all its fullness. Although mystery reminds us that our understanding of God always falls short of grasping him completely, the whole idea of his self-revelation in Christ was to show the truth in word and image. Again, for Daniel, his ability to deal with the poetic led him to uncover the meaning of mysteries. It led him to greater understanding of God and others on many levels, so that he could connect, translate, and reveal. A biblical embracing of mystery leads to more truth, not less: to wider knowledge; deeper understanding; more certain faith and hope.

A biblical embracing of mystery leads to more truth, not less

At the risk of over-simplifying, might it be that we have looked at evangelism as a *science* for much of the twentieth century and need to learn, in the twenty-first, to handle it as *art*? A number of experiments have emerged in recent years exploring a renewed application of creativity to the sphere of worship: with 'alternative' worship events incorporating not only music but visual and verbal art. Might it be time for the same movement to spill over into evangelism?

Poetic Jesus

Many commentators agree that there is a captivating, poetic quality to the ministry of Jesus, in contrast to the abrasive approach so often taken in our own culture. Amongst his many suggestions for ways in which the contemporary church can respond to the realities of a post-Christendom society, Stuart Murray urges us to re-evaluate the style of Jesus' earthly life and ministry, especially

- *Jesus, the unpredictable evangelist* – whose encounters with individuals were impossible to turn into a programme – encourages us to evangelise in ways that invite rather than pressurise and intrigue rather than overwhelm.

- *Jesus the storyteller and question-poser* – whose disciples were amused and perplexed by his sayings, whose opponents were disturbed by his provocative parables, and who pricked bubbles of pomposity and surprised outcasts with his acceptance – inspires us to renounce prosaic arguments and easy answers for dialogue, joyful exploration and openness to new insights.

- *Jesus, the unconventional political activist* – who threatened the establishment with his powerless authority, disappointed the zealots with his disbelief that peace could come through violence, questioned political agendas and gave political language new meaning and depth – challenges us to subvert the system for its own good and trust faithfulness rather than efficacy.

- *Jesus, the awkward dinner guest* – who ate so often with the wrong people that he was accused of gluttony, drunkenness and being a friend of sinners, and whose parables describe the kingdom as a feast with unexpected companions – calls us to inclusive table fellowship and cross-cultural hospitality.[71]

Might a more poetic faith lead to a more poetic evangelism; an appeal that far from shutting down the human imagination opens it up to the limitless possibilities of life in the service of a creative God?

One of the preachers I most enjoy listening to is Martin Young, pastor of Rising Brook Baptist Church in Stafford. Martin is an English graduate and has worked extensively in the theatre, including directing several plays. He has a beautiful, classical speaking voice that would not be out of place in the mouth of Sir Kenneth Branagh. He has a rich love of words. He embraces mystery and intrigue, and is passionately committed to the belief that it is possible, even in our complex and distorted world, to experience the love of God. Martin is a great preacher because he is poetic – in his approach to life and in his efforts to communicate. To listen to him is to be gripped again by the beauty of God; to be re-immersed in the loveliness of this faith that believes the best of every person and holds out the hope of healing to the worst of us.

He embraces mystery and intrigue

Martin's church is healthy and growing and there are any number of reasons for this. He has a great team around him; he and his wife are a dynamic duo; they are building on a well-laid foundation; the favour of God is evidently on the church. But one of the reasons for the church's growth – and an important one – has to be the presence, at its heart, of a passionate, creative, imaginative communicator who is himself overwhelmed by the beauty of the God he serves. Good communication is always at some level poetic. And good communication works.

Creative Engagement

If we are to allow the way we relate to the people around us to be shaped by a more poetic faith, as was the case for Daniel, we may need to see our understanding of 'evangelism' expanded to the much wider concept of 'creative engagement'. We have already seen, in our exploration of an acoustic faith in Chapter 2, that a new context calls for 'double-listening': we need to see now that this in turn becomes the cornerstone of mission. As we look, listen and learn in our culture, letting love shape our perceptions and our perceptions fuel prayer, we will find ourselves drawn into missionary response. As many have discovered through the 24-7 global prayer movement, there is nothing quite like *praying* for someone to clarify the ways in which God is asking you to *act* towards them. Creative engagement is born at the intersection of intimacy and involvement; of listening and loving; of passion and prayer. The walls of a prayer room, pinned to within an inch of their lives with names and photographs, poems and prayers, say more about the future of a church than any number of strategic plans. The fields into which God calls us with joy for harvest are more often than not the fields we have sown with tears in prayer.

When Elijah, at the end of his energies, engaged in such dynamic interaction he heard, broken though he was, the whisper of God: seven thousand were reserved in Israel for Yahweh and among them would be his successor, Elisha.[72] When Peter, overwhelmed by change and responsibility, engaged in such dynamic interaction, he heard the voice of God announcing the miracle of the gospel to a Gentile audience that would reach to the very ends of the earth.[73] One of the most common reasons for *not* seeing the blessing of God on our plans is that we don't wrestle for long enough at this first, creative stage. At

> One of the most common reasons for *not* seeing the blessing of God on our plans is that we don't wrestle for long enough at this first, creative stage

milestone moments in the history of salvation, both within and since the biblical period, new things have come to birth in passionate interaction with God and the culture *before* they have come to birth on the ground. Wholehearted, creative, passionate prayer is the maternity ward of God's mission.

When a group of us went to Prague two years ago for a 'Wholehearted' creative prayer weekend,[74] one of the participants offered to bring along disposal cameras for each of us. As we walked through Prague observing the city and praying for it, we were each asked to take pictures of images or settings that particularly struck us. Later that day, we had the pictures developed and each explained what it was that had drawn us to that particular image. The weekend had taken for its theme a single verse from the book of Revelation – 'And the leaves of the tree are for the healing of the nations'.[75] When we had each spoken of the pictures we had taken, the photographs were cut into the shapes of leaves and stuck onto an enormous tree that one of the artists had drawn out on paper. We then gathered to pray around this finished 'tree'. When we were later joined by believers from across the city, they were deeply moved to see prayers so physically and creatively set out.

The creativity and the passion of this shared act of prayer were unforgettable to all who took part. They turned prayer from a reluctant duty to a colourful dance; they enabled us in some small way to connect with the needs of Prague; they took prayer to a deeper level than most in the group had experienced. We have seen this same experience repeated on prayer trips to France and Croatia and with churches and youth groups in the UK, the USA and Australia. Different props, different places, different means of expression, but always the same theme of a physical, colourful, creative approach to prayer. Where art is allowed, in this way, to invade and transform prayer, the result is a potential revolution.

A passion that is born in the heart-felt prayer of creative engagement will lead to Christian mission that is marked by the three 'creative attributes' of *innovation, inspiration and imagination.*

Innovation

Innovation is essential to the development of new forms of Christian mission in our age. It is not enough that we are able to *think* creatively about mission, we need to *act* creatively and this will mean finding new ways to do old things and finding new things to do. The work of Al Hirsch and the Forge Network in Australia is one example of a movement that is fostering just this kind of creativity, with young leaders finding new ways to live out incarnational ministry in contemporary urban settings. Hirsch talks about the inspiration of the *Subterranean Shoe Room* in downtown San Francisco: a hyper-cool vintage shoe store created as a radical alternative to existing models of congregational church.

> Brock Bingaman is a Southern Baptist church planter/evangelist who came to San Francisco with every intention of planting a conventional purpose-driven type church. He had planted churches before and one conversation with him reveals that he is an evangelist to the core. But San Francisco is crawling with failed conventional purpose-driven type church planters. So secular, so culturally vigorous, so pro-gay is the city that the conventional churches are withering on the vine. Crestfallen, young Brock realized that there was no point trying to re-create what many had tried and failed at before

him. Needing gainful employment, Brock says he turned to his first love – shoes![76]

The result is a successful shoe store and a project that has given Brock and his team unprecedented contact with a whole range of people in the San Francisco scene.

'As a church planter, I spent ninety per cent of my time with Christians,' he moans. 'Now, as a shoe salesman, I spend ninety per cent of my time with non-Christians.' He has developed significant relationships with gay couples, Marxist professors, ageing hippies and bohemian artists. Just the kind of people you don't find in church. ... It's a tough town to evangelise, and Brock has struck on a natural way to incarnate the message of the gospel to a people group normally hostile to Christianity.[77]

In the approach to creativity that he invented and called *Lateral Thinking*, Dr Edward De Bono suggested that human beings have an overwhelming tendency to do the same things the same way repeatedly. So strong is this tendency that it becomes extremely so difficult to break out of established processes and patterns: like trams on a pre-determined track, we spend much of our time following the same well-worn ruts. It takes determination and effort to create and follow new thought patterns and in turn new patterns of action. But it is just this determination that is needed by the church in times of social change. Uncharted situations call for new ways of doing mission and the world is waiting for mission that puts innovation first. Novelty for

> We spend much of our time following the same well-worn ruts

its own sake has little value but novelty that responds to novel contexts has great worth.

Inspiration

A second vital element in creative engagement is *inspiration in lifestyle and leadership*. The first ever experiment in the use of electrical impulses to transmit signals (in what later became the telegraph) was conducted in 1746 by the French physicist Jean Nollet. Nobody had yet thought of wire as a conductive device, so the signal was passed instead along a line of seven hundred Carthusian monks. Each monk held an iron bar, also held by his neighbour. Monk number one was exposed to a stored electrical charge, and the impact on monk number seven hundred was measured. The result strongly indicated that electricity could be used to transmit signals – but short of laying endless lines of monks as national and transnational cabling, the benefit of the experiment remained untapped until the invention of wire.

The monks proved themselves to be supremely conductive: just as every natural material will either pass on an electrical charge or insulate against it. Copper and water are conductive, rubber and porcelain are not. The same experiment with seven hundred store-front mannequins would not have worked. In a similar way, in every culture or group, the 'charge' of creativity is being passed on or insulated against. Every leader either shuts down or opens up the creative potential of those they lead. We all either stifle or inspire. There are those who light fires, and those who carry buckets of cold water. The measure of a creative leader is not in the activity of their imagination alone, but of the imaginations of those they lead. How can we be sure that our leadership is copper-cabled – passing on the charge – not rubber-wrapped to kill it off?

As leaders we need to ask ourselves regularly whether our style and approach is freeing those we lead to pursue their own purpose and destiny, or enslaving them to ours. Are the groups and congregations we lead being inspired to reach further, to achieve more, to make the most of every gift and advantage they have been given? Or do they themselves feel discouraged and held back by our leadership style?

Daniel, for all else that he achieved as an individual, was clearly a massive inspiration to his fellow exiles. The stand made by Shadrach, Meshach and Abednego in Chapter 3 of the book of Daniel was brought about because of the stand made by Daniel in Chapter 1. With his infectious passion for the truth of God's ancient laws, he drew others into his sphere of action and influence; bringing out in them, in turn, a passion for God. Ask young leaders who have risked all to participate in God's mission in the world why they have done so: every one of them, at some stage in the conversation, will mention someone who inspired them. I would name Jill Tatman, Aunt

They urged me to aspire for more of God in my life

Dorothy, Don English, Richard Russell, Tom Sine, Mark and Carrie Tedder: people who brought out the best in me. They urged me to aspire for more of God in my life and opened my eyes to the breadth and majesty of God's work in the world. At a push, I could add another twenty names. These were not people whose job it was to inspire me: they inspired me because of their own passionate and creative response to the call of God on their lives. Their faith was eye-catching. They had the X Factor. By doing so creatively the things God had given them to do, they gave me the courage and the resources to up my own game. They had no idea, as they spoke to me, or prayed with me, or in some other way touched my life, that they were passing on a charge of electricity.

When was the last time you shook someone's hand and felt the emotional and spiritual equivalent of an electric shock?

Imagination

Lastly, creative engagement will require of us *imagination in communication and contact*. At the point at which the church meets the culture, where those who believe make contact with those who don't, is there an opening up of the imagination or are we closing down the very facilities our creative God can most work with? This is the area in which too wide a divide has been forced, I believe, between art and mission; between poetry and preaching.

The patron saints of creative engagement ought to be Bezalel and Oholiab, two little-known characters who played a crucial role in the development of the Hebrew vision of God. These were the craftsmen set apart by Moses, at God's direction, to oversee the creation and embellishment of the Tabernacle in which the first acts of corporate worship of Yahweh's newly-liberated people were to be held.[78] They were the first individuals in history to be specifically described as filled with the Spirit of God and they were artists. The tent of meeting was to be a creative, interactive, artful space in which the people of Israel would be immersed in a sacred and sensory experience of the presence of God in the world. To our eyes, it might well have looked more like an art installation than a church as we have come to view them. In our culture and context, such spaces would offer the opportunity not only of worship but of witness: they would be both the common ground and the holy ground on which those who appreciate beauty might make their first steps towards a greater awareness of God-consciousness.

Are we ready to harness all the gifts that God has given to his church in our attempts to show a jaundiced world his beauty? Are we willing to put the art back into the articulation of our faith? We have grown used to saying to our world that 'God is love.' Are we ready to say, with equal depth, that 'God is beauty'? There is a desperate need in our churches for a harnessing of imaginative power: celebrating creative gifts as servants of communication rather than of commerce. Art and architecture; poetry and plays; comic books and compositions: there are as many ways of firing the imagination as there are imaginations to be fired. Where are the young musicians and painters; the film-makers and dress-designers; the architects and city-planners who will take the love of God and neighbour and show the world what art-as-worship truly looks like? And where are the churches that will pray for them?

Where are the young musicians and painters

What does it take to set fire to the imagination of our culture? Imaginations that are on fire. What is the easiest, most natural, most creative way to communicate faith? To live an easy, natural, creative, faith-soaked life. It is not always easy to know exactly where to start but try this. Make a commitment to pray, at the beginning of each day, this simple, one-line prayer: 'Lord, set fire to my imagination.' Start looking for the ways in which God might be answering – and for the ways in which he might be urging you to answer your own prayer.

If God is able to do immeasurably more than all we can ask or imagine[79] … why not ask for more imagination?[80]

Love the words

Of all the poets who have awakened the poet in me, the greatest must be Dylan Thomas. I have been moved by his words on the page but much more by his own readings of his work, preserved in a series of experimental recordings by Caedmon Records. In Thomas I discern a love of art and beauty, a belief in the sheer power of poetry that inspires me deeply.

In her memoir of Thomas, *A Portrait of Dylan*, photographer Rollie McKenna recalls watching the poet as he directed the original cast of *Under Milk Wood* in New York

On a day of one of the last rehearsals before the first performance, I met Dylan and Liz in an Irish bar near the Poetry Centre. Dylan looked wan and worse than I had ever seen him. His speech was thick and he alternated between wild gestures and tearful blubbering. He said that he could not rehearse – not possibly. He could not even get to the venue. Desperate because we knew he wanted so much to make his cherished play a success in America, we cajoled and pleaded with him – but to no avail. We were at our wits' end as to how to help him and had given up when he gathered his wobbly round body together and said he thought he could make it. Relieved, we made our way uncertainly down the street and arrived safely. He vomited and passed out on the couch in the Green Room.

Meanwhile, the actors had come in. Liz shook Dylan awake; he muttered that he absolutely could not work. Yet, somehow, from some deep core of his being, he found strength to get up and put his cast through their most electrifying experience to date. I could not believe, as I photographed, hearing him admonish them to 'love the words... *Love* the words,' that he was the same man I had seen a few minutes before: a disoriented hulk had become a driving, inspiring teacher.

[At the first performance] ... the audience, not knowing at all what to expect, was quiet for the first several minutes. At last a few people tittered and then, realising that this was not an erudite work beyond their comprehension but an affectionately bawdy sketch of a village, everyone joined in the laughter that kept bursting forth until the curtain fell. Fifteen curtain calls later, Dylan came out alone. Only those in the first few rows could see the tears on his cheeks.[81]

An alcoholic and serious depressive, Dylan Thomas is hardly a noble role model for the Christian missionary of our century. And yet there is, in him, a passion for beauty that speaks volumes about God's creative touch. Like Peter Coard sketching the history of boot-scrapers, Thomas could not let the words and wonders of his childhood and heritage be lost. He was drawn to the beauty of words, transfixed by their God-given power to move and charm. This is the same energy that drives Rob Lacey, as he continues on his personal quest to bring Scripture alive for a new generation. It is the energy that has made Bruce Cockburn one of the most successful recording artists in Canadian history and an influence on millions the world over. It is the energy that inspired Steve and Lyn Taylor, founders of Graceway Baptist

He was drawn to the beauty of words, transfixed by their God-given power to move and charm

Church in Auckland, New Zealand, to turn Easter into an art festival and invite members of the local community to create their own responses to the theme of 'resurrection': creating an exhibition that was diverse and colourful, rooted in the community and rich with signposts to another kingdom, where resurrection is the rule, not the exception. It is the energy that inspires Christian artists, poets and musicians across the world to invest in creative projects that as often as not are unknown to the wider public.

Would that such a passion; such a creative energy; such a joy at God's simple beauties, could transform our grasp of mission in the opening fields of the century before us.

Psalm: You catch my eye

You catch my eye
In the eye of the storm;
You hold ointment appointments
When hell's hornets swarm.

When I find no time for stillness
You tell me there's still time;
When my words are clashing symbols,
You are reason,
Rhythm, rhyme.

You are the song that rises
In my soul;
You are the coin that clatters
In my begging bowl.

You are a bed of roses
On a crowded street;
A peppermint balm
To my blistered feet:

You are rich in rest,
When rest is radium-rare.
By cool pools you position me
With passion you petition me;
In fog and smog,
You re-condition my air.

You are the unexpected cheer
That lifts my game;
In the vinegar and lemon juice of life,
You are champagne.

Like a goat's milk bath
To Cleopatra;
Like honey on the throat
To Frank Sinatra:
You surround me to astound me,
You soothe and smooth.
You are the stalker
Who is good for me;
The jailer
Who can set me free;
The trap and snare
To bind me into love.

You who have refined me,
Come find me; mind me;
By grace grind me:
Bind me, gentle jailer, into love.

s t r e t c hing exercises

Trusting mystery

This chapter asserts that many people in our culture do not want the mystery of God *explained* to them: rather it is only in mystery that they can trust. Do you agree with this assertion? Is it true in your experience and in the conversations you have with others? If it is true, what difference might it make to the ways we engage in ministry and mission?

Consider the cross of Christ – the central mystery of the Christian faith. If you have access to a good image of the cross, take some time to meditate on it. How might you more fully engage with the mystery of this unique event? How might those you know who are seeking God be helped by having the opportunity to gaze, uninterrupted, on this mystery?

Engaging creatively

Consider the place of innovation, inspiration and imagination in your life of worship and witness. In which of these areas do you long for a more creative faith? Are there people you know and admire who model, for you, these important values? Are there others, in turn, who look to you as a model?

Ask God to bring to your memory each person who has inspired your faith in significant ways: who has 'lit a fire' in your life. Thank God for each one of them. Consider whether there might be some way of telling them of the inspiration they have been to you.

Ask God, in turn, to bring to your mind each person who is looking to you for inspiration. Explore how you might be, for them, someone who transmits the spark. Pray that God will never let you be the bucket of cold water that puts out the fire.

Ask God, finally, to help you act on the commitments you have made.

Psalm: You catch my eye

Take a few moments to read this poem. Do these images open doors in your imagination in helping you to embrace and explore God's presence in your life? How do they inspire you to think about your relationship with God?

Use the poem as a basis for meditation and prayer. If you feel up to it, try writing your own psalm, telling God in your own words what you think of him and what difference his presence in your life makes to you.

CHAPTER SIX

eccentric

Now when Daniel learned that the decree had been published, he went home to his upstairs room where the windows opened towards Jerusalem. Three times a day he got down on his knees and prayed, giving thanks to his God, just as he had done before (Dan. 6:10).

eccentric, *adj.* departing from the centre: not having the same centre as another, said of circles: out of the usual course: not conforming to common rules: odd… *Chambers Dictionary*[82]

eccentric faith: faith centred in a reality beyond the immediate

9³/4! Think you're being funny do you?

There is a very moving scene in the first Harry Potter film that captures, for me, the very essence of the story. It was a scene that had gripped me when I first read the book and it didn't disappoint me when Harry came to the silver screen. Setting aside for a moment any questions I might have about the impact of the Harry Potter phenomenon on young people's interest in witchcraft, this deeply redemptive scene explains, I believe, the profound and universal appeal of this story.

Harry has discovered that he is not an unwanted orphan but a wizard and that a place has been reserved for him at the highly reputed Hogwarts Academy. With his new friend, the giant Hagrid, he has been to buy all the things he needs for his first term as a wizard boarder. Now it is time **he is not an unwanted orphan but a wizard** to take the train. Harry's ticket tells him that he must find platform 9³/4 but there is no such platform. Between platforms 9 and 10 there is only a plain brick wall, and when Harry asks for help an unhelpful porter simply laughs at him: '9³/4! Think you're being funny do you?' Harry doesn't know what to do – until he spies another new pupil, Ron Weasley, heading with his brothers towards the same platform. Ron's mother kindly tells Harry how to get on to the platform he needs:

> 'Not to worry,' she said. 'All you've got to do is walk straight at the barrier between platforms nine and ten ... Best do it at a bit of a run if you're nervous.'[83]

Harry runs, pushing his luggage trolley ahead of him. But instead of hitting the wall, be goes straight through it, like a curtain on another world. He finds himself on platform $9^3/4$ of the same station, or perhaps it is not the same station. Everything is different; old-fashioned, comforting somehow. A painted sign indicates that this is the place for the Hogwarts Express and there the train stands: a locomotive from another age, steaming and gleaming like a scene cut from *The Railway Children*.

It is at this moment that we most starkly see the coldness of the known world: in the unpleasant cynicism of the platform porter, the brick-built logic of 9 and 10. In this world, ruled by the clinical inevitabilities of science and logic, there is no possibility of redemption. What will be will be. A child orphaned in terrible circumstances and locked under the stairs by a cruel uncle is destined to live out a meagre, mundane and uninspiring life: there is no hope of change. But in

This is a lush, imaginative world rich with the comforting flourishes of a bygone age

this new world of platform $9^3/4$, magic is possible. The story's end is not dictated by its beginning. In this other world, this world of which the poor deluded *muggles* have no knowledge, there is wonder and adventure, there are old myths to be spoken of and new myths yet to be created.

This is a lush, imaginative world rich with the comforting flourishes of a bygone age: a world of steam, not diesel; a world of wood, not steel. More St Trinians than Grange Hill, this is a world where house-points and school banquets replace identikit classrooms and chips-with-everything conformity.

This scene is, I believe, pivotal to the whole Harry Potter adventure. It speaks volumes to an audience trapped in the cold certainties of modernity; to people who are not entirely sure whether everything that there is to discover has already been discovered; to those worn down by cold cynicism and longing to believe in magic. It offers the hope of a doorway to another world. This is not a longing of our age alone. It is acute in our day because the 'modern' world-view has come totally to dominate our lives, but we are not the first to feel so trapped. In all human cultures, whenever a single, overarching system comes to dominate, when all our questions are answered for us and the possibility of creative alternatives is shut down there will be, somewhere within us, a longing for a different way. Albert Einstein famously stated that no problem can be solved by the continued application of the logic by which it was created. We know, deep in our souls, that we sometimes need to hear another voice.

Centred elsewhere

This is why, for all their strangeness, we are at times attracted to 'eccentric' people. At its root, the word eccentric doesn't mean bizarre or crazy. Rather, it indicates a life or a world-view that is 'rooted elsewhere', having a centre other than that chosen by the dominant system or world-view. People who are 'centred elsewhere' will call into question the assumptions of the age in which they live. In terms of the dominant culture, they will be both odd and at odds.

Sometimes their difference will indeed be rooted in madness, and words such as 'bizarre' and 'crazy' will legitimately describe them. But sometimes this will not be the case. Sometimes the logic they are centred in will be a deeper logic. The centre of their lives, odd though it may appear, might just be a better centre. Sometimes the world they point towards will be a better world.

Eccentricity, in this sense, holds out the hope of another world, the possibility of a different way. And Christians, by this definition, are called to eccentricity. We are called to live in Babylon; to be engaged; to be present; to be open to all that the culture has to say to us. But we are not called to be centred in it. Our centre is elsewhere, beyond time, beyond the immediate, in the very character of God. We are called to live in the creation, but to be centred in the Creator. In this sense of being 'centred elsewhere', *eccentricity* is one of the marks of Daniel's life. It is a thread that sets him apart from the first moment at which he leads his friends into a partial hunger-strike, and it is still with him when retirement from public life beckons. It is eccentricity, being centred elsewhere, that shapes Daniel's life and experience and it is this same eccentricity that arouses the jealousy, animosity and anger of his fellow civil-servants. *He is stretched between the reality experienced by those around him, centred on the idolatries of Babylon, and the reality of a 'different world' centred instead in the unchanging sovereignty of God's purposes.*

Dirty den

In Daniel Chapter 6 over sixty years has passed since the young Hebrews first came to Nebuchadnezzar's court. The fall of Babylon to the Persians, dramatically recorded in the 'writing on the wall' of Daniel 5, has made Darius the Mede

the city's effective ruler. Daniel is drawn out of retirement to
return to a prominent role in government and once again
the jealousies of his rivals are
aroused. The story follows in

Daniel defies an   many ways the pattern of earlier
order of the king   adventures, particularly that of
Shadrach,   Meshach   and
Abednego in Chapter 3. Daniel
defies an order of the king and is denounced by his
colleagues. He must face death – not this time in a furnace
but in a pit of hungry lions. Once again God's vindication is
seen in preserving his servant *through* the trial.

The parallels with Daniel 3 are strong and specific. In
both stories it is the angel of the Lord who comes (3:25;
6:22), in both the servants of Yahweh emerge unharmed
(3:27; 6:23) and in both the representatives of paganism are
killed instead (3:22; 6:24). The subtle difference that makes
this second story a complement to the first, rather than its
duplication, is the reason for the sentence of death. It is not
for refusing to worship idols that Daniel is singled out but
for refusing *to stop* worshipping Yahweh.

> Daniel's obedience flowed from his realisation that he
> would sin if he did not practice his own religion. In this
> way, it is the flip side of Daniel 3, where the three friends
> illustrated the realisation that they would sin if they
> participated in the false religious practices of their
> idolatrous oppressors. The two chapters together thus
> encourage later readers to avoid false religion and to
> pursue legitimate religion, no matter what the cost.[84]

Once again the response to the rescue is that the king
acknowledges the superiority of Daniel's God, issuing a
decree that the God of the Hebrews should be 'feared and

reverenced' throughout the empire. God has been proved in the time of testing and the result, yet again, is that Daniel prospers in the reign of this new king.

This is almost certainly the most famous of Daniel's adventures. It has bequeathed to us the abiding image of the prophet thrown into the lion's den, though the frequent Sunday school depictions of Daniel as a young man in this setting are mistaken: the text puts his age much closer to eighty than eighteen. The lions' den is an important chapter in Daniel's later life. The prophet who, as a young man, resists the power of an emperor by adopting a partial food fast is the same prophet who at the other end of a full and active life still finds the courage to stand for his God. From tenacious teenager to provocative pensioner, Daniel proves across the years that faith can thrive in exile.

Pick a window

But what is the key to Daniel's eccentricity? What enables him to maintain his 'centredness' so much that he can stand the plots and taunting of his peers and face the power of the king? What gives the weight to his life that empowers him to walk to the very threshold of the grave and yet not fear?

The answer is given in a second powerful image in this same chapter: a less known image perhaps, but a more significant one if we want to understand just *how* Daniel was able so convincingly to thrive in Babylon. It is the image of the old prophet, three times a day, kneeling at his open window to pray. His face towards Jerusalem, his heart toward Yahweh, Daniel demonstrates before a watching Babylon that he is 'centred elsewhere'. Prayer is the source and the substance of his eccentricity.

To what other direction should Daniel turn than to the Holy City, the place of his heart's desire, the focal point of his hopes and prayers for the progress of the kingdom of God?[85]

There are two key indications that this three-times-a-day pattern of prayer was well established in Daniel's life. The first is given in verse 10, where we are told that Daniel prayed 'just as he had done before', implying a pre-existent habit. The second is more subtle. It is that Daniel's enemies are so utterly convinced that the one thing that will catch him out is a law outlawing prayer to any man or god other than the king himself. The origin of this law is given in the text: it is set up specifically and deliberately to trap Daniel. His work record is just too good to allow any other approach. The king would not accept without evidence that his favoured servant had turned against him. The text implies that those determined to bring Daniel down must have known three key things about his life of prayer

- It was a consistent habit. There was a well-established and unbroken daily cycle, quite possibly a life-long habit. A month's ban would be easily enough to catch Daniel red-handed, because he is known to pray each day and every day. Prayer was hard-wired into his circuitry.
- It was a conspicuous habit. The window was always open. Daniel's prayers were not private, where the king might not see them: they were public; visible to all, and thus readily reported. It would be the easiest thing in the world to 'happen upon' Daniel just as he was praying and there would be no shortage of objective witnesses. There was nothing hidden about Daniel's life of prayer.
- It was a committed habit. Daniel was highly unlikely to break this pattern for the sake of the king's new law. His enemies perhaps struggled to understand *why* Daniel

was so wholehearted but they did not doubt that he was. The law was sure to catch him out because it was sure *not* to change him. Prayer, for Daniel, was non-negotiable.

Consistent prayer; conspicuous prayer; committed prayer – these factors make it clear that the habit around which this story revolves is neither short-term nor superficial. It is through prayer that Daniel finds a different centre to his life and through prayer that he maintains it. We are being introduced to a pattern that is deeply etched into Daniel's daily life; a pattern that marks him as surely as a hallmark shows the value of true gold and sterling silver, as thoroughly as a stick of

> Cut Daniel's life wide open and you will find prayer running through it

rock declares its resort of origin. Cut Daniel's life wide open and you will find prayer running through it. Trace his deeds and his decisions to their source, follow his moves and motivations to their starting point, all roads will lead you to the place of prayer. Like a homing device surgically implanted under Daniel's skin, it is prayer that always points towards the 'elsewhere' in which he is centred. In Daniel, prayer is both the measure and the mark of eccentricity.

This is a hugely significant discovery for our own journey through contemporary exile. Whatever else might help us through changed and changing times, the one thing we cannot do without is a commitment to pray. I have worked, over the past twenty years, with Christians from almost every known denomination, from free evangelical to Coptic Orthodox. Some are governed by worthy and ancient traditions: some are against anything more than twelve minutes old. Some are open to all manner of charismatic experience: some are closed to the least hint of it. Some love the church and can't get enough of meetings: others run from such obsessions and would rather just 'be' in the pub. Some find endless noise strangely attractive: others can only think clearly in silence. The range and variety of Christian 'brands' is mind-boggling. There's a flavour for every palate and a fashion for every personality. But I have discovered, in travelling and reading widely around the Christian community, that some things are essential, no matter which flavour you look to. One of these is love: there is little point in being a Christian without it. And another is prayer.

I have knelt as a card-carrying, tongues-speaking charismatic with my brothers and sisters who would run a mile from such a label and been overwhelmed by the passion and purpose of their prayers. I have moved from noise-rich Pentecostal worship-fests to silent, wordless contemplation and been utterly moved by both. I have prayed prayers invented on the spot and prayed prayers written centuries ago and found richness in each. I have shared in worship with artful Christians, musical Christians, word-centred Christians, power-and-ministry Christians, liturgical Christians and action-oriented Christians; and found in each setting a sense of God's presence. But I have never found a Christian, of any flavour, who can maintain a rich and rewarding faith without prayer. In one form or another a commitment to prayer, worked somehow into the routines of daily life, is essential to Christian discipleship.

Prayer is essential because it is through prayer that we make and maintain our centredness in God. Once we lose that lifeline our centre reverts, by definition, to the immediacy of the culture in which we find ourselves and we have no answer to the cold logic that declares all options closed and all hope lost. This is why the relationship was so quickly established, in 1950s Europe, between the philosophies of existentialism and the politics of despair and absurdity. Once you have no lifeline outside of the immediate, you have no source of hope. You are ruled by the immediate and trapped in its pathologies. Eccentricity is the key to hope – and prayer is the key to eccentricity.

Visibly eccentric – invisibly strong

The anger and confusion of Daniel's colleagues and competitors make it clear that they don't *see* what Daniel sees about faith in Yahweh. He is rooted in a reality that is invisible to others. The accepted rules of the culture, visible to all, cannot apply. Like a puppet pulled by invisible strings, Daniel must accept that his motivations will not always make sense to his peers. He has the courage to pursue a faith that, for all its invisibility to others, accounts for his strength and focus. In our own time, when freedom is proclaimed for all but dissent from cultural norms is cruelly denounced, this kind of courage must be at the heart of our faith. In a fluid value-system, the possibility of being misunderstood, accused of irrelevance or bigotry, comes with the territory of any firmly held belief. Daniel did not seek deliberately to be misunderstood. He was neither obnoxious nor obtuse: but neither did he fear misunderstanding as some kind of unthinkable fate. Can we expect faith to carry less risk of misunderstanding, in a culture whose refusal to hold to the 'eccentric' view that a Creator exists and burns with love for his creation, has led to cruelty and depravity on a scale unheard of in the annals of history.

The great crisis of humanity today is that it has lost its sense of the invisible. We have become experts in the visible, particularly in the West. If I were called upon to identify briefly the principal trait of the entire twentieth century, I would be unable to find anything more precise and pithy than to repeat again and again, 'Men have forgotten God.' The failings of a human consciousness deprived of its divine dimensions have been a determining factor in all the major crimes of this century.[86]

In the face of the confusion and corruption that self-centredness has brought and is bringing to our culture, a little eccentricity can be no bad thing. Is it time, in a world in thrall to the visible, the immediate and the comfortable, for a generation eccentrically rooted in the reality of an invisible God?

Privately eccentric – publicly strong

Although his open window clearly lets others know that he is praying, there is no indication that Daniel prayed thus as an act of public provocation. Like his earlier food fast, which was kept secret from all but a few chosen friends, Daniel's prayer life is a personal, private commitment. He does not hide his spirituality but neither does he flaunt it. It is these private resources, an inner life of discipline and renewal, which give to Daniel the strength to behave so differently in public. Eccentric prayer gives Daniel the discernment to think differently.

Daniel had amazing energy to discern and decide differently. Daniel had not let the contours of his life be submerged by the conventional definitions of the day. Daniel had maintained a capacity for alternative perception and therefore alternative action.[87]

Being 'centred elsewhere' has implications for the direction and flow of behaviour. The direction and lie of a ship's anchor will always be revealed in times of storm. Where we are *rooted* will largely dictate how we grow. A committed life of private prayer is more than a Christian duty or routine, it is a bedrock of the wisdom we will need to navigate the conflicts of a complex world. Is our culture crying out for people who can respond differently to life's storms because they are anchored differently in life's sea? God may ordain it that you should live in Babylon. He will never ordain that Babylon should live in you.

> **A committed life of private prayer is more than a Christian duty or routine**

The extraordinary attraction of irrelevance

The sting in the tail of Daniel's story; is that Daniel's life, in all its eccentricity, is oddly attractive to his pagan observers. Chief among these is Darius, Babylon's new Persian ruler. Darius is clearly in awe of Daniel. He has no desire to harm him and if it wasn't for the trickery by which he was cajoled into passing a law he cannot now repeal, he would gladly save him. Eccentric prayer bathes Daniel in the extraordinary attraction of irrelevance. He is centred outside of the immediate but this centredness arouses a potent jealousy in his colleagues. In our own culture, are there times when we are so keen to be *relevant* to our culture that we have forgotten how powerful a godly *irrelevance* can be?

The respect that Darius has for Daniel provides an intriguing twist to the narrative of the lions' den. Darius appears genuinely to favour Daniel and doesn't want to persecute him at all but he is trapped by his own pagan proclamations. He cannot rescind the decrees he himself has devised, so he must reluctantly put Daniel to the test.

It is possible, in this light, that the lions' den is not a means of execution at all but a test of integrity – the Babylonian equivalent of a medieval ducking stool. Subjects of the king who are suspected of disloyalty or deception can be 'locked in' to this ultimate test. If 'the gods' preserve them, it is a mark of their integrity. If they die, this proves that they deserved to. It

the Babylonian equivalent of a medieval ducking stool

may be that Darius, far from wanting Daniel dead, is looking for a way out of his dilemma and resorts to this ultimate test in the desperate hope that Daniel *will* survive. This possibility is suggested by the wording of the story in several places, not least in the fact that it is the king himself who rushes to the lions' den after an allotted time has passed to find out if Daniel's God has preserved him. It is also Darius, not Daniel, who prays to Yahweh for the prophet's deliverance. Daniel himself does not, at any stage of the incident, pray that God will save him. His trust is in God and he is content to go forward on that basis. Darius, though, is more nervous of the possible outcome. As his Prime Minister is lowered into the pit of already hungry lions, moments before the stone is rolled across the only possible escape, he says to Daniel

'May your God, whom you serve continually, rescue you!'[88]

Daniel is being punished for breaking a decree by which prayer to any man or god other than Darius himself is utterly outlawed. But the last words he hears before the stone rolls into place and he has only lions for company are the words of the king *breaking his own decree*. Is it any wonder Daniel trusts in God to rescue him? Need he even pray for deliverance when Darius, the pagan king in whose name the might of Babylon has been crushed, has done it for him? Such is the attractive power of Daniel's eccentricity. The king himself – the very man who should most be outraged by his servant's insistence on being 'centred elsewhere'– is drawn to pray to Daniel's God. This is the hidden power of an eccentric life. When your centre is not only outside the immediate culture but is in fact found in the very centre of the universe, the ultimate centre of all that is, there is a good chance that your life will be attractive to others. It may arouse jealousy and envy, or it may arouse aspiration and curiosity. It will not arouse indifference.

One of the people whose eccentricity has most influenced my thinking in recent years – as it has many others – is Pete Greig. The founder of the 24-7 prayer movement, a global tide of prayer he 'started by accident', Pete has for many years been committed to an eccentric view of prayer. Unlike many in his generation, he refuses to dismiss prayer as 'uncool'. He knows and understands the cynicism of his age but he will not let his faith be smothered by it. Instead, he is open in his passion; innocent in his hope; unafraid to pray towards goals that are unrealistic and, by all rules of logic, unachievable. Like many visionary leaders, Pete is followed by a perpetual mist of organisational chaos, like the *Peanuts* character Pig-Pen taking his dust-cloud wherever he goes. But in the chaos there is creativity and energy, and Pete has been an inspiration to Christians across the planet.

The 24-7 prayer rooms that have sprung up across the UK and the world in response to the visionary leadership of

Pete and his team are not logic-driven meeting places for strategic thinkers. They are places of inarticulate passion, for people who don't know what the best strategy is and aren't sure they ever will, but are content instead to throw themselves on the mercy of God and cry to him for change. They are creative places, where prayer is expressed as often in music, art, poetry, movement and silence as in the more recognisable spoken form. They are places where the simple act of taking someone's name and pinning it to a noticeboard begins, somehow, a chain of change. They are places, very often, where the eccentric plans of a God who is, by definition, centred elsewhere collide gloriously with the eccentric longings of a people open to him. What Pete has understood, I think, about passion, is that you can't harness it too tightly. To some extent you have to hang loose, to leave room for outcomes you may not have foreseen. There is a place for order and for planning. Strategies do matter but the landscapes of the future are 'chaordic'.[89] They demand that the creative energy of chaos be wed to the need for order. 24-7 is perhaps the best example yet seen of a chaordic Christian response to the needs of twenty-first century culture. And it is run, almost exclusively, by eccentrics.

In and through Death's curtain

Daniel at the open window is as significant an image of his life as Daniel in the pit of lions. The latter might tell us of his faith and courage, his resilience in the face of death and his capacity to trust his God for rescue. But the former tells us where these strange gifts come from. They are rooted in the prophet's eccentricity, in the fact that he is 'centred elsewhere'. Daniel knows that there is another world beyond the visible. He knows that Babylon and Persia do not have the last word. Caught between the Platform 9 of Babylon and the Platform 10 of Persia, facing the unyielding brick wall of competing totalitarian systems before whom he is a powerless mite whose God is neither known nor feared; confronted by the terrible choice to deny his God or die: Daniel opts for the platform $9^3/4$ of prayer. Courageously, faithfully he walks straight at the wall and death becomes a curtain in his path.

It is hardly surprising that so many commentators have seen in this story the prefiguring of the resurrection of Jesus. Jesus faces the ultimate test – the 'lions' den' of death itself – as a stone is rolled across his tomb to mark him dead. By all the rules that guide our world he should stay dead. But Jesus lives by other rules. He knows there is a 'deeper magic'. The stone is rolled away as a new sun rises and he is found to be alive. He has faced, and passed, the ultimate test. He is the one whose God

Jesus faces the ultimate test – the 'lions' den' of death itself

> '… is the living God and he endures for ever; his kingdom will not be destroyed, his dominion will never end. He rescues and he saves; he performs signs and wonders in the heavens and on the earth …' (Dan. 6:26,27)

Resurrection is the ultimate eccentricity, the final statement of a life that is 'centred elsewhere'. Death itself cannot make its logic hold when these new rules are cited. Though all the world's unhelpful station porters might scoff, 'Resurrection! Think you're being funny do you?' The new reality stands. Why would anyone not *want* to be rooted in the 'deeper magic' of this new world?

s t r e t c hing exercises

Centred elsewhere

Does the idea of being 'centred elsewhere' hold meaning for you? Of all the Christians you know, who are the ones who seem to you to have this sense of being rooted in God, unfazed by the changing circumstances of their lives and culture? Is theirs a life you aspire to or would not want? What gives them their sense of centredness?

Ask God to show you how strong your 'centredness' in him is. Again, don't go searching for a guilt-trip but be open to the areas in which you are more centred in the immediate culture than you need to be. Richard Foster suggests that the three 'classic areas' for this are in our handling of money, sex and power. As you examine your heart, ask God to show you if there are connections to be broken and habits to be healed. Pray – and act – accordingly.

Prayer

Consistent, conspicuous, committed – do these three words describe your devotional life? If not, how might you deepen your experience? Think about three concrete, practical questions:

When is God calling you to pray? In the mornings? In the evening? During a lunch-break? On one particular day of the week? What is the best pattern for you to find new windows for prayer in your life?

Where is God calling you to pray? At home? At work? On a walk, run or cycle ride? At the gym? In the cathedral? What would be the best, most helpful and most fruitful place for you to put yourself to pray with more consistency and commitment?

How is God calling you to pray? Alone, with your partner, in a small group? Using books and guides or with only your own imagination? Following a pattern or scheme? Using the Lord's Prayer as a framework? Keeping a list of those you pray for or recording a prayer journal? Is God calling you to deepen your daily habit of prayer or to undertake a special exercise – a retreat day or pilgrimage; a 24-7 experience?

Pray for a deepening of your life of prayer. Ask God to show you the how, where and when. Pray for inspiration and resources. Ask God to bring to mind the names of others with whom you might pray. Make a commitment to taking at least one initial step, no matter how small and act on it.

CHAPTER SEVEN

panoramic

*In my vision at night I looked, and there before me was one like
a son of man, coming with the clouds of heaven. He approached
the Ancient of Days and was led into his presence. He was given
authority, glory and sovereign power; all peoples, nations and
men of every language worshipped him. His dominion is an
everlasting dominion that will not pass away, and his kingdom
is one that will never be destroyed (Dan. 7:13,14).*

panoramic, from **panorama,** *n.* a wide or complete view: a
picture disposed around the interior of a room, viewed
from within in all directions: a picture unrolled and made
to pass before the spectator… *Chambers Dictionary*[90]

panoramic faith: faith that sees its future in the light of
God's global plan

House of Tyres

Fifty-nine-year-old Mike Reynolds is no ordinary architect. Time was he would sit for hours in his self-built 'meditation pyramid' receiving visions and instructions from visiting spirits or 'wizards'. These days he is more likely to attend a conference on energy efficiency and sustainable technology in home building. His major contribution to architecture, the 'earthship', was at first dismissed as an idiosyncratic and impractical dream. It started out as a hippy experiment in alternative living. It has evolved into a possible template for the housing of the future.

The 'earthship' is the name Reynolds has given to the houses he has developed and built in many parts of America – there are an estimated one thousand in existence around the world. Looking like a cross between a Mexican pueblo, a greenhouse and a **A favourite building material is old tyres** Hobbit's cottage, earthships are built into a hill-side, with south-facing glass walls to make the most of every moment of sun. They have two distinctive features. Firstly, they are constructed entirely of recycled materials, much of which would otherwise be land-fill. A favourite building material is old tyres: packed with earth, stacked like bricks and plastered over, tyres make the perfect building material, according to

Mike Reynolds. The second, perhaps more significant feature of earthships, is that they are 100 per cent self-sufficient in energy. Warmed by the sun by day, they benefit from the thermal energy of the earth that surrounds each of their rooms on three sides, as it releases that same day's heat back into the house through the night.

> They can be built just about anywhere. They don't need to be connected to any utilities and they don't harm the environment, nor do they require any significant sacrifice in terms of living standards, unless you're fond of long showers. They are heated by the sun, generate electricity from solar and wind energy and catch rain water from the sky. They process their own sewage through plant beds, which also provide fresh bananas all year round. ... Once built, earthships cost virtually nothing to run.[91]

Reynolds is fond of quoting one of his New Mexico clients, who says of her two-bedroom earthship that the lowest temperature experienced was 69°F (21°C) while the highest 76°F (24°C). Her total utility bill for a year was $47 (£25).

The significance of these facts is not simply that some people who don't mind taking short showers are able to save money: it is that these houses are built in the light of the future. Reynolds speaks of his creations as 'independent vessels to sail on the seas of tomorrow'. They are houses built for today with the day-after-tomorrow in mind. This is a man who has a stark and vivid vision of the future and in the light of that vision is prepared to live out a very different present. To some he is an ageing hippy who won't give up his dreams. But to others he is a prophet, with a thriving six hundred-acre development in New Mexico, emerging projects around the world and enough credibility to have held, in 2004, the world's first 'Earthship Summit' in Brighton.

Dreams of tomorrow

Reynolds illustrates in the sphere of architecture a principle that holds equally true in other spheres of life: that our hopes for today will be deeply shaped by our vision of tomorrow. The future throws its shadow back into the present. The way we see our future will affect the way we interpret present events and will change the expectations and aspirations that shape our daily lives. This is perhaps particularly true in the arena of faith, which tends towards a future focus. For Christians the very essence of faith is, as Roy McCloughry has expressed it, 'living in the presence of the future.'[92]

The future throws its shadow back into the present

This is without doubt the understanding that the Book of Daniel is asking us to adopt. The first half of the book is made up of the six stories whose significance we have considered in the preceding six chapters. Even in these narrative sections, there is an emphasis on dreams and visions of the future. Nebuchadnezzar's dream of a four-storey statue and Daniel's interpretation of it, are foundational texts in the genre known as *apocalyptic*, a term applied to 'any book purporting to reveal the future or last things.'[93] When it comes to the latter half of Daniel, starting with Chapter 7 and running to the end of Chapter 12, narrative is all but abandoned and the book focuses almost exclusively on a series of apocalyptic visions. These concern the immediate, mid-term and long-term future of the Hebrew exiles. Tremper Longman III suggests that six major themes, introduced in the stories of Daniel 1-6, reverberate through the prophetic visions of Daniel 7-12

- The horror of human evil, particularly as it is concentrated in the state
- The announcement of a specific time of deliverance
- Repentance that leads to deliverance
- The revelation that a cosmic war stands behind human conflict
- Judgement as certain for those who resist God and oppress his people
- The equally certain truth that God's people, downtrodden in the present, will experience new life in the fullest sense

These visions become the 'big picture' against which we are asked to understand and interpret the experience of exile. There is always a danger that exile will produce a 'shrinking' vision of life. The Hebrews are deprived of military victory, settled land, royal status, public worship and political freedom. Their horizons are limited to day-by-day survival. But it is here that Daniel discovers the 'bigger vision' of a future-liberating kingdom. Behind this vision is the strong assertion of the sovereignty of God over the world. Kings may *appear* to have the power to crush God's people, empires may *appear* huge and unstoppable but appearances can be deceptive. Behind the scenes the sovereign God is working out his purposes and his people, in due course, will see their fulfilment. *Daniel's faith is stretched between the micro and the macro: between the everyday experience of the life he is called to lead and the deeper, wider certainty he holds of God's promised future.*

From there to here

Daniel 7 is the bridge between the earlier, narrative portions of the book and the later vision-based material. It is set some fifty years into exile, in the reign of Belshazzar, who was the son of King Nabonidus and ruled over Babylon as his co-regent for ten years. The chapter in many ways parallels Chapter 2, where Daniel was able to unlock the dream of Nebuchadnezzar. Here we are offered an account of Daniel's own dream, in which visions of the future are described.

Daniel was able to unlock the dream of Nebuchadnezzar

- Nebuchadnezzar's earlier dream described four successive kingdoms in terms of the four sections of a great statue, and looked to a further, final kingdom that would overcome all others and last for ever.
- Daniel's later dream also describes four kingdoms, this time as four beasts rising from the sea. Again a further, godly kingdom arises. This is an everlasting kingdom, superseding all others and offering security to the saints of God.

This later vision confirms the apocalyptic nature of the book of Daniel and introduces the five final chapters, which further explore these themes in a series of dramatic visions. But the clear parallels between the dreams of Chapters 2 and 7 confirm that even in the 'story' elements of its first half, the book of Daniel is apocalyptic and prophetic in nature.

Daniel's capacity to thrive in exile can be partly attributed to his grand vision of the future. So convinced is he of God's ultimate sovereignty, he is prepared to live out his own life in patient service, knowing that the people of God, whether now or in a future generation, will ultimately experience the fulfilment of God's plans. The New Testament book of the Revelation of John, which draws heavily on the imagery of Daniel, fits the same purpose for the new-found Christian communities of Asia Minor. Facing persecution and growing uncertainty about the immediacy of Christ's return, the new churches are looking for a platform on which to build their faith and to engage with the Greek and Roman worlds. John provides this in the bold assertion that, be it sooner or later, Christ will return and all the kingdoms of the world will be 'wound up' at his coming. He anchors the faith of the New Testament church in future certainties, like an investment broker banking on the markets of tomorrow. These realities, for John as for Daniel, are as real as this morning's news headlines, as solid as the history unfolding around us.

The message of both Daniel and John is the same: if you base your faith only on the realities you see *here and now*, you will flounder and lose hope. But if your anchor sinks deep into *God's future promises*, it will hold you through the worst of storms. Apocalyptic visions deal in ultimate events: global-scale developments marked by a cosmic finality. Against the perspective of these events our present circumstances, our temporary trials and short-term struggles take on a different light. The evil shadow of the empire that has hovered over us, blocking out the sun, seems to lose its power. Even if we die in its grip, we die knowing that its days are numbered. The earth-eating machinery of the global system that oppresses us, that seems so strong and permanent and unbeatable and cruel, seems a little less tall against the scale of God. Apocalyptic visions are about a change of perspective, about the camera of our lives panning out to see the bigger picture and our own place within it.

At the heart of the visions of Daniel, as of John, is the kingdom that is coming, the kingdom that will destroy all others; that will last for ever; that will give to the poor and the humble and the righteous a place at the very banquet table of God. But these visions are not intended to leave this kingdom as a future hope. They are intended to convince us, now, of its reality. They are intended for our encouragement, our empowerment in this present dark age. This is the unique gift of biblical faith, that it offers a God's-eye view of the past, the present *and* the future. It uniquely allows us to situate ourselves in the bigger picture of God's plans for his creation.

The power of knowing

Several years ago a group of behavioural psychologists in America conducted an experiment on the effects of noise on the concentration levels of workers. Volunteers were asked to complete a series of tasks, with various levels of noise played in the background. Sounds ranging from traffic and machine noise to the voices of people and animals were blended together to create an irritating background clamour. The key to the experiment was that half of the volunteers were given a switch on their desk enabling them to turn down the volume of the noise or to switch it off altogether. The rest had no way of doing so. As predicted, those with the switch showed much higher concentration levels than those without. They

> **But here's the twist in the tail: none of these volunteers *used* the switch**

were better able to complete their tasks and complained less about the distraction of the background noise. But here's the twist in the tail: none of these volunteers *used* the switch. They were so caught up in their tasks that they didn't get around to switching off the noise and yet the presence of the switch increased their productivity.

The conclusion drawn from this experiment was that *having control* improves human performance even where *control is not applied*. If we know we have a handle on our circumstances and environment, we will feel more secure and concentrate better than if we feel we are hapless victims of annoyances beyond our control. The importance of this assertion to our vision of the future is that the same is almost certainly true of *perspective*. If we are able to see in perspective the trials we are passing through, this is likely to have a positive effect even if nothing in our circumstances changes. The future can impact the present even though it hasn't happened yet and doesn't actually change the conditions we live under.

Imagine you live in a beautiful valley that has been all but destroyed by the traffic on a six-lane motorway built through it. You have campaigned against the intrusion; picketed government offices locally and nationally; produced endless statistics proving the ill-effects of the tens of thousands of cars that pass your home hourly. Even as you crusade and campaign, the traffic just gets heavier. You wonder if there will ever be a change. Then you are leaked a copy of a secret government report. This proves beyond doubt that there will be a global oil crisis within ten years. Statisticians predict a reduction of up to 90 per cent in traffic levels within fifteen years. The government is already making contingency plans. Everything changes. The most important question in your life becomes 'Is the report reliable?' Once you know that it is, the focus and direction of your campaigning shifts. You no longer need to 'win' a fight against the cars because their fate is now sealed. What you now know about the future changes everything about your experience of the present. Knowing how the story ends changes the way I play my part today.

Thus I can live with the absence of God's healing as I raise my hands to worship the God who will come one day to dry every tear and heal every infirmity. I can tolerate the weight of injustice because I know that the tidal wave of justice is on its way. I can bear the burden of oppression because I know that freedom is coming, as sure as dawn follows night. I can live with my own incompleteness, knowing that completion is promised. This doesn't stop me from reaching out for healing; from railing against injustice; from seeking freedom; from wrestling with the sin that resists my completion. I yearn for these things because I do want to know more *now* of the reality of God's future reign. But in my yearning for these things, I am not frightened that they are victories I will never see. I do not fight as one who expects, ultimately, to lose. I know that God has set in motion the forces of liberation; that he has released resurrection into the created order, to run with its muddy boots all over death's plans for us; that he will bring to fruition every good work of redemption that he has begun. So I am able to live in patience and hope, accepting the *'not yet'* of the kingdom as fully as I accept the *'now'*.

Participation in God's dream

The message of the book of Daniel is that a passionate vision of God's intended future is integral to the faith we profess now. The future has a role in our lives and the darker the days we live through, the more important that role becomes. Seeing God's future enables us

- *To know beyond doubting that behind the events of our age the sovereign God is at work.* Daniel's visions are of future, distant events but they unroll in the context of a known present. Time and again these visions make a link

The future has a role in our lives
between the events we *see* and the forces we *don't see*, working behind them. Like Dorothy peeking behind the curtain to find the Wizard of Oz projecting his great delusion, Daniel allows us to see behind the everyday events of our world. A vision of the future offers us *perspective*.

- *To know the depth and splendour of the inheritance that awaits us.* Daniel is no doubt as to why this coming kingdom matters, or what our part in it might be. This is the kingdom that God will give to his saints – this is their destination and their destiny. Like the will and testament of a rich old uncle, signed and sealed and waiting only for delivery, this promise is certain and secure, naming in its deeds the saints of God: 'Then the sovereignty, power and greatness of the kingdoms under the whole heaven will be handed over to the saints, the people of the Most High. His kingdom will be an everlasting kingdom, and all rulers will worship and obey him.'[94] Our God-given perspective on the future becomes the source of our expectations and of *hope*.

- *To pray and work for the revelation of God's kingdom.* Once we know that the kingdoms of this world will not stand; that there is a coming kingdom of righteousness and truth; that the final pages of history are already written, we know where our priorities should lie. Our efforts and energies will not be invested in the passing systems of Babylon; they will be poured into this coming kingdom: looking for it; expressing it; celebrating it; helping others to see and know it. The hope we have creates a *focus* of our lives.

- *To face the false powers of our age, whatever they might be.* The perspective given to us by these future visions gives us, in turn, the courage to face the bully-boy empires of our age, whether political, industrial or commercial. We come to understand that they are not, after all, the ultimate winners. Their days are numbered. Their judgement is already on its way. Nebuchadnezzar, Belshazzar, Darius – we need not fear them, because no matter how hugely they project their shadow, the empires they build will not stand. The new-found focus of our lives becomes our source of *courage*.

- *To be strong in faith, passionate in prayer and free in worship.* This perspective on God's future, this picture of a world where all ends well in the power and the presence of a loving Creator, this certainty of redemption and renewal for our planet: this vision is not something to be shelved for future reference. It is a thing to be celebrated and welcomed, an energy that runs through the everyday world. We are energised by our participation in God's dream. The perspective that fuels our hearts with hope and expectation, that shapes the focus of our lives, that gives birth to courage in the face of evil and becomes in turn the fountain and the flavour of our *celebration*.

Get the hope without the hype

Three important observations need to be made about apocalyptic literature and the realities of living in the light of the future. The first is that these visions matter more for their content than their style. It has been easy for Christians through the ages to be fascinated by the graphic presentation of these visions. The comic book imagery of Daniel and Revelation, with their beasts and battles, their number codes and cryptic dating systems, have provided successive generations with endless opportunities for speculation and fear. Our own time and culture has been marked by such imaginings. But the essence of these books does not lie in their population of many-horned beasts, it lies in their message: God wins!

The second important observation to make in this context is that the Bible's apocalyptic visions, including those of Daniel and John, are always intended to be read in the light of the wider witness of Scripture. Daniel refers to the prophecies of Jeremiah and clearly situates his visions in this wider setting. John, in turn, draws references from Daniel's text. Distortions and misinterpretations are always more likely when apocalyptic texts are read in isolation and applied to a given cultural context without first having been weighed against the Bible's total view.

Distortions and misinterpretations are always more likely when apocalyptic texts are read in isolation

Thirdly, it is important to note that apocalyptic visions are global in scope. They give us a wider view of geography and culture, as well as a deeper view of history. These visions are planet-wide in their intent: they speak of the ultimate destiny of the cosmos and all creation is drawn into their scope. All kingdoms, all rulers, all people – all that God has made he will redeem. The end that is promised is the end of *all things*. Human cultures and people groups from every time and place will be included in God's future. This means that we should be careful not to apply these visions too quickly to a specific time and culture or to see a particular nation or people group as the centre of God's purposes. And it means we should look forward to celebrating the great feast of God, when people from every tribe and ethnic group will gather and the voice and song of every language and tongue will be caught up in the worship of the God who has won the final prize. Daniel's visions place his experience of God in the wider context of this bigger picture. He sees the big-screen picture of God's purposes but knows, too, that his small-screen contribution matters. He is globally connected and locally engaged. God is the God of the whole earth and is at work throughout the world. His global plan **How many of us** validates my local action. We **stand in need** can't expect to understand our place in God's world unless we at least begin to see the world from God's perspective: recognising the importance of all its tribes and families; rejoicing in its many colours and cultures; knowing the unique significance of each individual life. Nor will we understand our place in history without seeing history through God's eyes. How many of us stand in need – against the confusion and complexities of our culture and the small-mindedness of so many of our churches – of a bigger vision of God's work in the world?

The certain vision of God's promised future will shape our behaviour in the present in a number of key ways.

For example, if we know that a day is coming when God will call his servants from every tribe and tongue and nation to celebrate his victory together, we may want, now, to get to know the diversity of human cultures. Where those cultures know nothing of the promise of God for their future, we might feel the compulsion of God to be among those that will tell them. As the patchwork of God's purposes comes together, each culture contributing its own special colour and design, we might ask God what part we play. Is there a particular people group for whom we are called to pray and act? Is there some special part of the picture to which we can contribute? If, in turn, we see in our own congregation or denomination a preponderance of one or other culture we might feel motivated to push at the boundaries; to seek diversity; to invite others in and to look for our brothers and sisters in other streams and stand side by side with them.

For example, if we know that a day is coming when God will wipe away every tear and heal every pain, when justice will roll out like a river and drive the very essence of injustice into a pit of fire, might we not feel motivated, when we hear the cry of the oppressed, to tell them what we know? Might their suffering not spur us to stand with them, to declare together that justice is eternal and injustice a passing phase? If we know that Babylon is temporary, that God will reclaim the ground he has created, might we not feel called to *tell* someone?

For example, if we know that the very make-up of the coming kingdom is love; that kindness will be its watchword and beauty its obsession; that the poor will find rest and the weak relief; that 'Love and faithfulness meet together; righteousness and peace kiss each other'[95] might we not want to align ourselves, now, with love and kindness, to work at righteousness; to embrace peace; to value faithfulness? Might we not desire even now to fill our lives with the things that will last into that coming kingdom and to empty our lives of that which will be lost? If greed is a commodity whose stock value is falling, would we not want to rid ourselves of greed? If envy and bitterness have a limited shelf-life, would it not make sense to ditch them both? Knowing something of what the future holds won't solve all our problems, nor will it absolve us of hard work and personal effort but it will give us some sense of how our efforts should be channelled. Ask any stockbroker – the investor who knows what the future holds is not guaranteed overnight riches but they do have an excellent lead in knowing where to invest.

Freedom at the Café Gondrée

God has a dream for his creation and those who have heard and followed his voice become part of the delivery of that dream. A popular image that has often been used to describe the 'now but not yet' nature of God's kingdom is the image of living in occupied territory, waiting for our day of liberation. Europeans – raised as we have been on the mythic movies of the twentieth century – will often imagine this in the context of Second World War France. The occupying army ensures that the local population are not free to enjoy the fruits of their own land, even though they are at home within it. This resident population, especially those who resist the occupier's values and goals, must accept a loss of privilege, a relative poverty, a range of restrictions in social functioning. They must live as 'exiles' in their own homeland. It is not that their home is elsewhere but that their home has been rendered an alien place. Despite the fact that they are living in a place that in historic terms is rightfully theirs, they must live as if it wasn't and express their resistance through underground relationships and clandestine activities: knowing, hoping, believing that one day liberation will come and the land will once again be made home.

They must live as 'exiles' in their own homeland

As colonies of resident aliens, the local groups of New Testament Christians were the cells of a resistant movement – an underground network dispersed throughout the empire, living as citizens of Rome and yet knowing, in reality, that their true identity was different – that they were citizens, rather, of a coming kingdom. No picture of this status has ever been clearer to me than that

of Georges and Therèse Gondrée, proprietors of the Café
Gondrée at Benouville in Normandy.

The Café Gondrée is set in a small, detached house on the
banks of the ship canal that runs from Ouistrahem, on the
Normandy coast, to Caen, a few miles inland. In 1944 the
café was owned and run by Georges and Therèse Gondrée,
whose daughter Arlette is the current owner. It is adjacent to
Pegasus Bridge, the only crossing of the canal between the
coast and the city. In the planning for D-Day, the Allied
Command knew that this bridge was crucial to the success of
their invasion. They had to know that they could hold it
before the troops were landed on the beaches. Accordingly,
the commandos of the Sixth Airborne Division were
dispatched in gliders to secure the bridge, six hours before
the Normandy invasion began. They landed in fields adjacent
to the bridge and took and held their target, with two-thirds
of them losing their lives in the ensuing battle. The Café
Gondrée, the only building in the immediate vicinity of the
bridge, was too close to be ignored and was liberated along
with the bridge itself. Thus it was that for six hours, from
shortly after midnight on the night of June 5th to dawn on
the morning of June 6th, the Gondrée family were the only
family in France to be liberated. Their café carries a plaque to
this day declaring it to be the first house in France freed from
German occupation.

It would be hours before the battle for the Normandy
beaches began and months before the whole of France was
free: but in the meantime Georges and Therèse Gondrée
enjoyed the exhilaration of freedom. No one else yet knew
what they knew, nor saw what they saw but this did
nothing to change the reality. Liberation was on its way
and they could taste, even now, the first fruits of its coming.

This is the church to which we belong – the community
of the first fruits of the liberation God has launched. The era

we live in, whether it proves to be a two thousand years or a twenty thousand years span, is lived entirely in the six hours between midnight on June 5th and dawn on June 6th, in the hallowed freedom of the Café Gondrée. We are 'resident aliens' because an occupying force has sought to rob us of our inheritance but we are a people of promise because that force has been given notice to quit. The Holy Spirit is God's down-payment, poured out to us so we will know,

The Holy Spirit is God's down-payment

in quality and quantity, that everything has changed. The kingdom we belong to – the 'land' we will call home – is both arrived and arriving, both present and promised. It is the ground beneath our feet and it is the rumour of freedom brought to us on the evening winds. We live out our exile knowing that our future is secure.

I have visited the Café Gondrée on several occasions, at first as a tourist and later as a pilgrim, and it has become hallowed ground in my life. There is something here about Britain and France, about Europe and the promise of liberation that touches me very deeply. If you are ever passing the hamlet of Benouville, on the road from Ouistrehem to Caen, I urge you to take a short detour to Pegasus Bridge and the Café Gondrée. Take a few moments to pray and ask God to show you, in the depths of your being, what the first fruits of liberation are to be in your life and what it means to share with others the life-changing news that the occupation is over.

In the café itself, with its dark wood counters and tables and its fading photographs of Georges and Thérèse Gondrée, there is a sense of humanity that thrills me. The Gondrées were not happy because they had in some *theoretical* sense been 'saved', they were happy because their actual lives – their down-to-earth, all-too-human, coffee and croissant lives – had been saved. And so it is for us. Liberation is not a theoretical saving of our lives, accounted for in the distant halls of some inaccessible heaven: it is a here-and-now, grounded-in-reality redemption of all that we are and hope to be. It is in our humanity that we are freed and it is to all humanity, with its longings and leanings, its dreams and desperations that the promise of salvation is offered. We are exiles in the inhumanity of Babylon but we wait, like children on the eve of Christmas, for that which is truly human to be born.

The Taming of the Truth

Like a football match
Where the fans are locked out
While the players take turns
On the terraces
To cheer

Like a concert
Where the crowd sits in silence
While the band
Play through headphones
So that only they hear

Like a hospital
That keeps itself
Germ-free and sterile
By only treating patients
Who aren't sick

Like a spoonful of sugar
With no medicine

Like a mule
Without a kick

Like an ocean liner
On a pleasure cruise
Purely for the pleasure
Of the crew

Have we taken what was given
As a message for the many
And made of it
A massage
For the few?

s t r e t c hing exercises

Living in the light of the future

What difference does God's promised future make to the life you live now? Take some time to reflect on this question in your own life and circumstances. How might the future that God has promised us change the decisions we make day by day in our lives? How are your ambitions and aspirations changed by knowing how God will end the story, even if you don't know when?

Pray that God will give you insight into the future he has promised for the church and for the world and that you will have the courage to live now in the light of that future.

A multi-coloured, multi-cultured, patchwork celebration

If God's future involves celebration and worship drawn from every tribe and tongue and nation, how does that affect your worship *today*? Are there ways, starting now, that you can celebrate and anticipate the coming day? Are there ways in which your church can join with others to affirm God's multi-coloured plan? Do you need to challenge the cultural bias of your church?

Ask God to give you a vision of the world as he sees it, in all its richness, colour and diversity. Ask him to show you how this richness might be brought more fully into your church. Create space for silence and ask God to bring to mind specific people you can contact or steps you can take to express publicly

God's love of colour and diversity. Repent where you need to.
Commit to new attitudes and actions.

First fruits of liberation

What are the signs of the kingdom in the life that you lead?
Where do you see the 'first fruits' of liberation? Find a pen
and paper and create some space for reflection and imagine
you have been asked to give an interview for a popular
magazine. They have heard that you are a Christian and
that Jesus is spoken of as a 'liberator' in our lives. They have
asked you to suggest to them key ways in which you have
experienced liberation, in which you are experiencing
liberation and in which you hope to experience liberation in
the future. They want a candid and honest interview. What
are the areas of your life that you will talk to them about?

*Make the notes you have jotted down for this exercise the subject
of reflection and prayer.*

*Where have you experienced the liberating presence of Christ?
Take time to thank God for his salvation.*

*Where do you still need to experience God's liberating power?
Invite the risen Christ to come into this area of your life and in
his way and in his time to bring you into freedom.*

*Where are you looking forward to the full freedom that God's
final acts of redemption will bring? Thank God for the certainty
of the hope he gives.*

CHAPTER EIGHT

conclusion

'As for you, go your way till the end. You will rest, and then at the end of the days you will rise to receive your allotted inheritance' (Dan. 12:13)

Chocolate Church

The film *Chocolat*, based on the best-selling novel by Joanne Harris, ends with an Easter Morning sermon by the parish priest, Pére Henri. The young priest is eager to connect with his parishioners in a way that the traditional, ascetic Catholicism of Lenten observance has not. As the camera pans across the congregation we see the characters we have come to know in this most turbulent of villages; characters caught up in the ebb and flow of life and love, always in the shadow of the ever-present church. We see the Count, whose efforts to defend traditional values have brought him into conflict with the villagers' new sense of freedom; whose own most careful life has recently begun to unravel and who until today was the unseen writer of every word the priest would preach. We see the conflict and resignation in his eyes as his erstwhile protégée departs from the pre-determined script

We see the conflict and resignation in his eyes

> I'm not sure what the theme of my homily today ought to be. Do I want to speak of the miracle of our Lord's divine transformation? Not really, no. I don't want to talk about

his divinity. I'd rather talk about his humanity. I mean, you know, how he lived his life here on earth; his kindness, his tolerance. Listen, here's what I think. I think we can't go round measuring our goodness by what we don't do, by what we deny ourselves, what we resist and who we exclude. I think we've got to measure goodness by what we embrace, what we create, and who we include.[96]

Essentially a twenty-first century debate projected back into a quasi-1950s setting, *Chocolat* is about the place of food, sex and other pleasures in our lives and the struggle of the church to embrace these most human of delights. Pére Henri represents a view of faith that is able to connect with the desires and aspirations of ordinary people, and thus to survive in an environment in which sheer frustration threatens to drive these same people from the church. The film, like the novel on which it is based, is ambiguous towards organised religion. It can't quite decide whether faith is a helpful or a harmful ingredient in the cake of life and it therefore offers two competing versions of the church. But it serves to illustrate an important aspect of faith that is all too easy to forget in the rush to win converts and build churches: that mission is as much about being human as being Christian.

It's not Terry's, it's mine

The 'presenting pathology' of the church depicted in *Chocolat* and personified in the life of the dysfunctional Count is that it has nothing to say to the human concerns of ordinary people. The church tries its best to reach and teach the people but it can make no connection with the ordinary concerns of their lives. It tells them how to be good Christians but never how to be good humans. It asks them to love God, who is distracted and distant, but never teaches them to love each other. It calls for the curbing of their appetites, but never speaks of the fulfilling of their aspirations. This is contrasted in the film to an earthy, sensual, chocolate-loving paganism; a 'faith' that meets people where they are; that celebrates life in all its variety; that places freedom above faith.

Behind these contrasts and criticisms lie the prejudices of the story's author, Joanne Harris. In this and her many other books she makes no secret of her disdain for organised religion, of her suspicions of Christianity and her fascination with paganism and of her evident commitment to fun, food and freedom. But her criticisms are not without foundation. All too often the church *has* failed to dignify and sanctify the ordinary, to give significance to human questions, longings, cares and concerns. The God of the Bible, by contrast, shows no such indifference. The God of Daniel is the sovereign God, King over every heart and every home, concerned with every detail of our lives. This is the God who lays claim to every sphere of our interest and influence, who seeks the

> All too often the church *has* failed to dignify and sanctify the ordinary

throne not of our church but of our world. This is the God for whom, as Abraham Kuyper so often wrote, there is not one square inch of the universe over which he does not cry 'This is mine, this belongs to me.' Far from being indifferent to our humanity, far from ignoring the concerns of our everyday lives, this God is the One who sends us out to *transform* the everyday. God wrestles for the Lordship of the ordinary. Like a heavenly Dawn French holding the chocolates of the world to her chest, God looks lovingly over the sum total of human experience and says 'It's not Satan's, it's mine!'

One of the Christians who has most encouraged me, over the years, to live out a truly human discipleship, is Andy Thornton. An accomplished songwriter and performer, Andy was for a number of years the Director of the Greenbelt festival. The festival seeks to walk a line between being a Christian gathering and being an arts festival that any audience, Christian or not, can enjoy. And it seeks to embrace a passionate and heartfelt commitment to God's justice in the world. Andy gave excellent leadership to this movement because he embodies in his own life these same concerns. He is passionate in his love for God; he has written or co-written some of the most moving worship songs I heard in the twentieth century. Some of the songs he wrote for Glasgow's *Late Late Service* several years ago were played so often in my car that I all but wore out the tape. And he is passionate, too, in his love for humanity. He is a people person, and will never let religion – his or anyone else's – get in the way of the simple, unadorned expression of love and tolerance. And he is passionate in his love for God's justice. As a singer, as a social worker, as a campaigner, as a Christian leader Andy carries a fire of love for the poor. All this I have seen in a man who is gentle, loving, committed, creative and faithful. I'm not sure that Andy has ever thought of himself as a hero and I doubt if he has any idea of the extent to which he has inspired others but he is one of the people whose attitude and demeanour has had an impact on my life.

As far as I know, it was Andy who came up with the name 'Humanic' for Greenbelt's youth programme. It may not have been but he can have the credit anyway. It's a wonderful word which speaks of energy and passion, of the sheer joy of being human. It is a word that captures, for me, the very essence of the Christian faith. Jesus did not come to deliver us from our humanity but to bring fulfilment to it. Faith is the fulfilment of human aspiration.

Book-ends in the everyday

It is for this reason that it is so important that the book of Daniel begins and ends in the ordinary. Though Daniel lives through some experiences that are beyond extraordinary, his adventures are book-ended by the everyday. His interaction with exile begins with the everyday decision of deciding what to eat. The journey that will ultimately lead him to stand before kings, that will impact empires and shape history, begins with a vegetarian diet. As a Jew, Daniel knows that obedience is for the ordinary. God's laws are not given only for temple worship and sacred assembly.

God's laws are not given only for temple worship

They are given for health and hygiene, for work and worship; for commerce and community. It is precisely *in* the outworking of everyday life that the distinctive obedience of the Hebrew faith is made real. The high points of Daniel's public life that are recorded for us in this narrative are interspersed with long periods of mundanity: periods when Daniel was living out his life, distinguishing himself in his career, serving where he was called to serve and by implication maintaining a vibrant life of daily prayer. The special moments of Chapters 2, 4, 5 and 6 are separated by great lengths of the ordinary, like towns on a long highway with vast tracts of desert in between. If the book of Daniel were a play in six acts, the intervals would outlast the action a hundred to one. Again by implication, it was in these long spells that Daniel proved the true resilience of his faith. He would not have been called upon to read the writing on the wall if he had not been known as a man of integrity and truth. He would not have been so focused before the lions if he had not been so faithful through the long haul of the preceding sixty years.

The last words of the book of Daniel confirm, if there was any doubt, that the prophet is called to an ordinary life. This final 'book-end' in the life of Daniel is a remarkable key to the understanding of a long-haul faith. After the stories of trial and triumph, after the long life of faithful service, after the dreams and visions of a future in which the sovereign God wins all, Daniel is told by an angel, quite simply, to *get on with his life*

> 'As for you, go your way till the end. You will rest, and then at the end of the days you will rise to receive your allotted inheritance' (Dan. 12:13).

Eugene Peterson, in *The Message*, translates the angel's words as

> And you? Go about your business without fretting or worrying. Relax. When it's all over, you will be on your feet to receive your reward.[97]

The promise is of a future kingdom – a future resurrection. There is an inheritance to come. But the immediate call is to perseverance and faith: 'go your way till the end'; 'Go about your business'. An old man perhaps tired of waiting for the fulfilment of the dreams his God has given him, Daniel is sent, in effect, back into exile. It is in the 'here and now' reality of Babylon that he must press on to the very end.

Deliverance is promised but the promise is not yet delivered. Just as Daniel has lived his faith in the ordinary more than the extraordinary, by a factor of a hundred-to-one, so he is sent now *back into the ordinary*. The kingdom he has seen is a 'now but not yet' reality, and until it is revealed there is no world to live in but the real world. God has lifted the curtain on the future but it is in the present that faith must be applied. It is the commonplace, routine realities of Babylon that the promise of the kingdom will transform.

Into exile

This parallels a significant conversation between Jesus and his disciples in the pregnant pause between resurrection and Pentecost, between the proving of God's victory and the coming of his power. Just as the angel calls Daniel to faithful witness, so Jesus offers to his disciples both the certainty of the kingdom that is coming and the challenge of the life that must be lived until it comes. Convinced that this must be the moment when the kingdom foreseen by Daniel will be established, with the Messiah taking up his throne in Jerusalem and the world sitting up and taking notice, the disciples ask 'Lord, are you at this time going to restore the kingdom to Israel?'[98] Jesus replies

'It is not for you to know the times or dates the Father has set by his own authority. But you will receive power when the Holy Spirit comes on you; and you will be my witnesses in Jerusalem, and in all Judea and Samaria, and to the ends of the earth.'[99]

You *will* receive power, and you *will* be my witnesses: but it will be in the here and now, in exile, as resident aliens in all the places to which my Spirit sends you. The kingdom of God is promised: the sovereignty of God in history guarantees it. There is a day coming when exile and alienation, trauma and trial will be no more. But that is the *not yet* of God's kingdom. The *now* is a world waiting for the touch of God's grace, a world deep in thrall to false gods, deep in the darkness of injustice. The *not yet* may be extraordinary; subsuming the cold world of platform 9 and 10 once and for all in the glorious, colourful, idiosyncratic, Platform 9³/4 world of the kingdom but the *now* is ordinary and everyday, a world of *muggles* in need of revelation and healing. The *now* is Babylon. The power of God is given for your exile.

You *will* receive power, and you *will* be my witnesses

> Amidst our complex modern societies God calls his people still to bring a kingdom perspective to bear on the totality of their lives and to resist the idols of the day.[100]

All the aspects of faith that we have highlighted through this book – the intrinsic, acoustic, elastic, kenotic, poetic, eccentric, panoramic ways of following God that will help us to thrive in times of exile – are given for the transformation of our ordinary lives. They are given that we might be more fully human, that we might live a life worth living, that wisdom and wonder might flow through us like streams through a desert. In the final analysis the greatest achievement of Daniel's life was that he *lived*; fruitfully, creatively and passionately. Daniel proved that it was possible to live in exile and to live well. He kept the dream of God's future alive. He explored and expanded his people's understanding of God's plans. He challenged pagan kings. And he walked, one step after another, one day at a time, through over sixty years in exile. He saw his ordinary life transformed by the worship of an adventurous God. He saw the everyday enlightened by God's presence. No exile is beyond the scope of God's blessing because every place is given to us to be transformed. Every place on which the foot of the believer falls is open for redemption, invited to join in God's great adventure.

The Humanic Gospel

This view of faith as a key to human fulfilment can transform the way we approach evangelism in our day. It enables us to build mission on a platform not of difference but of shared humanity. At the heart of evangelism is the assertion that conversion to Christ will make a difference in the lives of those who follow him. Believers are, in that sense, not like the unbelievers around them. If there is no difference, conversion has no meaning and evangelism no goal. But in our efforts to communicate this truth, we have succeeded very often in establishing not only *difference* but *distance* from those to whom we speak. Our

If there is no difference, conversion has no meaning

evangelism consists in sketching out the great gulf that has opened up between the believer and the non-believer, between the before and the after of conversion. So convinced are we that conversion will produce a radical and comprehensive transformation that we project the view that everything will change. 'Nothing that you are now will remain with you after this decision is made' and 'Nothing that you will be is yet present in your life.'

This is the very opposite of Paul's approach in Athens. Despite facing a people with whom he is utterly unfamiliar and has little in common; despite being privately disgusted by their idolatry; despite being unable to use any of the language with which he was most at home (the language of prophecy and promise, of Jesus fulfilling the age-old longings of the Jews), despite all this Paul makes it his business to *establish common ground* with the people to whom he is speaking. He relates directly to their spiritual search; he commends them for the very idolatry that sickens his heart; he quotes their poets and he introduces them to a God who is already, though they don't know his name, present in their worship. He proclaims a God whose offspring they are. Paul uses the term 'we' to express the common destiny of all humanity. He understands that because he is a Christian he is in some sense different from his listeners, and that the differences matter. But he also knows that because he is human he is the same as them.

The suggestion that Paul, in his faith, is both 'the same as' and 'different from' his audience is the paradox that lends creative energy to his preaching. He establishes common ground, but having established it he is quick to tell his audience that he knows something they don't. There are aspects to God they have not yet seen and their Creator will one day judge them according to his criteria, not theirs. Paul stands on common ground with the people of Athens but from the place where he and they stand he points towards a place they have neither seen nor been. He seems to have grasped the deep truth of effective communication – that people will not listen to you unless you are somehow the same as them but that they will have nothing to listen to if you are not somehow different. Common ground is established in the expression of our shared humanity, and from that ground a new and unfamiliar word is spoken.

Just as Daniel was engaged but distinctive in the foreign cultures of Babylon, so Paul presents a message in Athens that is at one and the same time both familiar and new.

Two important things are happening to the gospel message at this moment, perhaps for the first time. The first is that Paul is expressing an explosive and world-changing truth: that Jesus is the fulfilment not only of the longing of Israel but of the longing of every human heart. It is not only Jewish temple worship that has tried and failed to reach God through sacrifice and now must learn to approach through Jesus. The same is true of every other act of worship in which the human longing for communion with God is expressed. Every human aspiration, every human culture and every human cry is met and fulfilled in Jesus, the Creator's loving response to his lost creation.

The second is that the possibility of response is opened up. If Paul had emphasised the difference and distance between himself and his audience, then the conclusions he had drawn about Jesus would not be valid for them. If you and I are substantially different people, then the answers you have found to life's questions may well have no meaning for me. The gospel might simply be, as it is so often described by those outside the church, 'OK for people like you, but not for me.' If, on the other hand, you and I are substantially the same, standing on the same ground, asking the same questions and sifting through the same evidence, then your conclusions may well have meaning for me. I am compelled more by shared humanity than by difference.

Authentic evangelism is not the announcement that Jesus is the answer to the question I once asked – it is the announcement that Jesus is the answer to the questions you are now asking. The gospel speaks to human concerns, it answers human questions. It is God's response to the cry of the human heart. Can we envisage an approach to evangelism that expresses common ground more deeply than difference? Are we able to begin with the everyday human concerns of those around us: to answer the questions they are asking rather than cajoling them to ask the questions we are answering? Following Jesus is the best way, the only way, to be fully human. It is a road that welcomes the aspirations and longings of every human heart and converts our desires until we see that they are fulfilled in Christ. Is it time that the church that claims to follow the Creator began more fluently to interact with his lost creatures?

The gospel speaks to human concerns, it answers human questions

The Prismatic Church

Here is a vision of a God who will transform the world through ordinary people putting obedience and worship at the centre of their ordinary lives. Each believer, in this view, becomes a channel through which God can pour blessing into a world in need – like the places on an engine through which oil can be applied. God pours *through his people* the healing he dreams of for the world.

The mechanics of just how this might take place are revealed in the writings of the Apostle Paul. Paul articulates a vision of the church as a community of liberation, the first fruits of God's reign, bringing the touch of divine love to a world of need and loss. The outpouring at Pentecost, with each person receiving the fire of God and carrying it with them to the furthest corners of the Roman Empire, becomes for Paul a sophisticated and substantial vision for the life of the church. In the letter to the Ephesians that vision is set out in detail. Two key verses offer a way into this sky-wide vision of a church that touches the whole world. In Ephesians 3:10, we are told of God's plan:

His intent was that now, through the church, the manifold wisdom of God should be made known to the rulers and authorities in the heavenly realms, according to his eternal purpose which he accomplished in Christ Jesus our Lord.101

The image is that of a prism. As the pure light of God's wisdom hits the church, in all its variety of ages, races, cultures and genders, the light fragments into a million colours, making visible the height and the depth, the length and the breadth of God's love. The church, a collection of those who are seeking to follow Christ, becomes the means by which these God-colours are carried to every corner of the world. Because the church is made up of people from every walk of life, every walk of life gets a share of God's light. The spread of liberation is viral: those who are infected pass it on. In Ephesians 4 we are given the second key to this remarkable puzzle:

It was he who gave some to be apostles, some to be prophets, some to be evangelists, and some to be pastors and teachers, to prepare God's people for works of service, so that the body of Christ may be built up until we all reach unity in the faith and in the knowledge of the Son of God and become mature, attaining to the whole measure of the fulness of Christ.102

God has given gifts to the church to provide for its leadership, growth and development. It is to be a dynamic, living body: expanding, growing, deepening its faith. And every one of those gifts, whether apostolic, prophetic, pastoral, instructive or evangelistic, is to be harnessed to one central purpose: to equip God's people for the tasks of service to which they each are called. It is as the members of Christ's body find and fulfil the works of service God has called them to that the many-coloured wisdom of God is made known. These are not predominantly works of service *in* the church, though some no doubt are. For the vast majority of people, they are works of service in the world. They are the behaviour that demonstrate a kingdom difference; loving where others might hate, working with a passion because work is worship. They are our acts of studying and designing; our creating and exploring; our caring and teaching and building homes and communities in which the love of God and of neighbour are core values.

The church plays its part in bringing the blessing and wisdom of God to the whole creation by equipping each of its members to live out the fullness of their calling. As we each find and develop the gifts God has given us and take our place in loving and blessing the poor we come more fully to understand just which corner of the creation God is seeking to redeem *through us.* As I embrace my vocation I discover in my God-given purpose the key to fulfilling my potential.

The teaching of the *equipping church* will genuinely shape the Christian mind. Its ministry will challenge, build up and heal the individual. Its networks of friendship and mutual support will connect believers to others in the same field and calling. Its worship will inspire and empower each believer to make a difference in their small world.

The church is, above all, an agency of equipping, tasked with releasing the people of God into their God-soaked role as the heralds of healing for the world.

Some people complain that the notices are the most tedious part of any church service. But I dream of a church where there are so many notices that there is no time for anything else. I dream of a church where every spare inch of wall space is covered with notice boards; where there is so much to announce that even the

Some people complain that the notices are the most tedious part of any church service

ceiling is used for the small-ads. I dream of such a church because I dream of a setting in which God's people are being encouraged and equipped for redemptive tasks in every sphere of everyday life; where there are so many different football teams up and running that a new member is spoilt for choice; where there are prayer meetings for dentists and think-tanks for nurses; where teachers meet to talk together of the kingdom possibilities in their schools; where people who have known success in business take time to mentor and equip the unemployed; where artists and photographers and DJs and web designers seek each other out to create vital sparks of prayer and interaction. The list could go on forever, as long as the world itself. Not that all, or even any of these activities need be based in the church itself but I dream of a church so obsessed with equipping its members for real life, so overwhelmingly sold on the vision of a gospel that transforms the ordinary that it serves as a kind of Piccadilly Circus for vocation and mission, a creative, chaotic machine that thrusts people out into their callings almost as quickly as it has drawn them into worship.

The church is called to a prismatic role, receiving the pure white light of God's wisdom and dispersing it to every corner of the culture. Paul's vision validates the role of the church both as a gathered and a dispersed community. When we gather, it is so that we might be strengthened and equipped for our dispersal. The gathered church is the engine room of the social transformation that the church in dispersion makes possible. There is a church *beyond* the congregation, but there is no church *without* the congregation.

The Home Stretch

On this journey with Daniel into exile, we have identified seven factors of faith that seem to have enabled the Hebrews to thrive in Babylon:

INTRINSIC faith: so deeply rooted it shapes everything.

ACOUSTIC faith: grounded in the learned art of listening.

ELASTIC faith: stretched but not broken by adversity.

KENOTIC faith: expressed in servanthood and self-emptying.

POETIC faith: opening the imagination to God's beauty.

ECCENTRIC faith: centred in a reality beyond the immediate.

PANORAMIC faith: seeing its future in the light of God's global plan.

In our own post-modern exile, can these same seven factors offer us the edge that Daniel clearly enjoyed? Can they lift us beyond a limited and limiting commitment to survival, to see how we might thrive in these new times? Might we find, as the tide-lines and prevailing winds of our evolving century cut deeper and deeper into the landscapes of our lives, that a new seed of faith is growing: that somewhere deep within us a new heart is taking root?

Let me come clean about my own assessment of these questions. I have been called crazy for believing it but I have can only answer 'Yes.' I don't believe that western culture has seen the last of Jesus Christ. I don't believe that the failing and falling façades of Christendom will be the lasting memorial to the Son of Man in our history. I don't accept that God will slide gently into the night and leave the cultures

I have been called crazy for believing it

whose heart and soul he has so shaped to journey on without him. I believe, rather, that hope will be reborn in the lands that were once 'Christendom'.

Towards the end of 2004, I was listening to a religious service on the radio in my car. The reading was from the prophet Zechariah, speaking of the restoration of a people who had known exile. 'Just as you, people of Judah and people of Israel, have been a curse among the nations' the prophet declared, 'so I will now save you, and you will become a blessing.'[103] The ancient words rang out to me in the context of contemporary Europe: addressed as they were to a people who had once known God's blessing, had lost it and were given the promise of renewal. We are neither Judah nor Israel: our context is different. But how these words echo in the Europe of today. Europe, whose blessing of industrial growth gave the world the curse of environmental disaster, whose dream of human equality created communism and murdered millions, whose sexual revolution turned Aids into a global epidemic. Holocaust, apartheid, unbridled consumerism; all evils that grew from seeds planted in European soil.

We are not alone in bringing harm to the world but we share the blame. European culture has blessed the planet but it has also cursed it and there are millions today throughout the world whose lives would not be so blighted if it wasn't for ideas forged and decisions taken here in Europe. The challenge to the church is two-fold. Firstly, are we willing to wrestle for the Christian heart of Europe. Do we have the courage and confidence to tell all who will listen that the faith *matters* to us and that we believe that it should matter to our culture? And secondly, are we prepared to believe that God can save Europe, so that our continent can once more be a blessing to the nations? Is this too big a hope to carry? Has exile stolen from us the capacity to dream God's dream of a world made new? Or will we dare to believe in God's future for our culture? To pray for it; to look for it; to each seek our place in its emerging streams? To sing God's song in this strange land?

God grant us a faith that will stretch to face this challenge.

> We are not alone in bringing harm to the world but we share the blame

References

1. *Chambers Twentieth Century Dictionary* (Edinburgh: W. & R. Chambers, 1972)
2. Tony Benn, *Dare to be a Daniel* (London: Hutchinson, 2004)
3. Martin Robinson and Dwight Smith, *Invading Secular Space* (Crowborough: Monarch, 2003)
4. J. B. Phillips, *Your God is Too Small* (Touchstone Books, 2004)
5. A term used extensively in the twentieth century by John Stott and others.
6. Luke 18:8
7. Hebrews 11:2
8. *Chambers Twentieth Century Dictionary* (Edinburgh: W. & R. Chambers, 1972)
9. Ray Bradbury, *Fahrenheit 451* (Voyager, 2004)
10. Stuart Murray, *Post-Christendom: Church and Mission in a strange new world* (Carlisle: Paternoster, 2004)
11. With grateful thanks to Anna Robbins for her thoughts on this.
12. Proverbs 29:18
13. Daniel 2:14
14. Isaiah 42:3
15. Matthew 12:20
16. Matthew 10:42
17. John Holdsworth, *Dwelling in a strange land: Exile in the Bible and in the Church* (Canterbury Press, 2003), p.19
18. Mike Riddell, *Threshold of the Future: Reforming the Church in the Post-Christian West* (London: SPCK, 1998), p.55
19. Ezekiel 2:9–3:2

[20] See Craig Bartholomew, Consuming God's Word: Biblical interpretation and consumerism, in *Christ and Consumerism: A critical analysis of the spirit of the age,* Craig Bartholomew and Thorsten Moritz Eds. (Carlisle: Paternoster, 2000), p.89

[21] Henri Nouwen, *The Genesee Diary: Report from a Trappist Monastery* (Doubleday, 1976), entry under Friday, August 2nd.

[22] Jim Wallis, Christian Values and the Three Poverties, The Second Temple Address, 2002, published in David Hilborn, Ed., *Movement for Change: Evangelical Perspectives on Social Transformation* (Carlisle: Paternoster, 2004), p.164

[23] *Chambers Twentieth Century Dictionary* (Edinburgh: W. & R. Chambers, 1972)

[24] Tremper Longman III, *The NIV Application Commentary: Daniel* (Zondervan, 1999), p.84

[25] Jurgen Moltmann, The Church in the Power of the Spirit, cited in Roy McCloughry, *Living in the Presence of the Future* (Leicester: Inter-Varsity Press, 2001), p.166

[26] Rob Lacey, *The Word on the Street* (Zondervan, 2002)

[27] Dewi Hughes, *Castrating Culture: A Christian Perspective on Ethnic Identity from the Margins* (Carlisle: Paternoster, 2001), p.221-223

[28] Dewi Hughes, *Castrating Culture: A Christian Perspective on Ethnic Identity from the Margins,* Paternoster, 2001, p.188

[29] Viv Thomas, *Second Choice: Embracing Life As It Is* (Carlisle: Paternoster, 2000), p.119

[30] Acts 17:22,23

[31] 'He who answers before listening – that is his folly and his shame.' Proverbs 18:13

[32] John Holdsworth, *Dwelling in a Strange Land: Exile in the Bible and in the Church* (Canterbury Press, 2003), p.27–32

[33] Revelation 21:3,4

[34] Psalm 84:6

[35] Ajith Fernando, *What should we be doing now? Some biblical reflections*, a message to the Church in Sri Lanka (Sri Lanka Youth for Christ, January 2005)

[36] *Chambers Twentieth Century Dictionary* (Edinburgh: W. & R. Chambers, 1972)

[37] John E. Goldingay, *Word Biblical Commentary: Daniel* (Carlisle: Paternoster, 1989), p.76

[38] Lawrence O. Richards, *Expository Dictionary of Bible Words* (London: Marshall Pickering), 1985, p.114

[39] Psalm 137:4

[40] Psalm 46:1–7

[41] Psalm 87:1–7

[42] *Chambers Twentieth Century Dictionary* (Edinburgh: W. & R. Chambers, 1972)

[43] Cited in Dewi Hughes, *Castrating Culture: A Christian Perspective on Ethnic Identity from the Margins* (Carlisle: Paternoster, 2001), p.170

[44] Dave Andrews, *Christi-Anarchy* (Oxford: Lion, 1999)

[45] Alan Storkey, *The Politics of Jesus*, manuscript, 2004

[46] Tremper Longman III, *The NIV Application Commentary: Daniel* (Zondervan),1999, p.145

[47] Philippians 2:5–11, Eugene Peterson, *The Message* (NavPress, 2004)

[48] Walter Brueggemann, *The Prophetic Imagination* (Fortress Press, 1978), p.95

[49] Isaiah 42:16

[50] George Austin, Archdeacon of York, quoted in Cowley, *Going Empty-Handed – The true source of spiritual power and authority* (Crowborough: Monarch, 1996), p.79

[51] Ian Cowley, *Going Empty-Handed – The true source of spiritual power and authority*, (Crowborough: Monarch, 1996)

52 John 19:10,11

53 Ezekiel 17:24

54 Viv Thomas, *Future Leader* (Carlisle: Paternoster, 1999), p.176

55 'And if you spend yourselves on behalf of the hungry and satisfy the needs of the oppressed, then your light will rise in the darkness, and your night will become like the noonday' (Is. 58:10).

56 Matthew 10:39; Matthew 16:25; Mark 8:35; Luke 7:24

57 Matthew 20:28; Mark 10:45; John 6:51; Philippians 2:6–8

58 Bamber Gascoigne, *The Christians* (London: Book Club Associates, 1977), p.16,27

59 David Bosch *Transforming Mission: Paradigm Shifts in Theology of Mission* (New York: Orbis Books 1991), p.193

60 John Holdsworth, *Dwelling in a Strange Land: Exile in the Bible and in the Church* (Canterbury Press, 2003), p.76

61 Matthew 25:35,36

62 Psalm 17:8, 'Keep me as the apple of your eye; hide me in the shadow of your wings.'

63 *Chambers Twentieth Century Dictionary* (Edinburgh: W. & R. Chambers, 1972)

64 Peter Coard, *Vanishing Bath* (Bath: Kingsmead Reprints, 1973)

65 Walter Brueggemann, *Finally Comes the Poet: Daring Speech for Proclamation* (Fortress Press, 1989), p.3

66 Brian D. McLaren, *The Church on the Other Side: Doing Ministry in the Post-modern Matrix* (Zondervan, 2000), p.89

67 Cited in *The NIV Application Commentary: Daniel* Tremper Longman III (Zondervan), p.142

68 Jack, Miles, *Christ: A Crisis in the Life of God* (London, Random House, 2002), p.3

69 Acts 17:22–31

70 Psalm 78:2; Matthew 13:34,35

71 Stuart Murray, *Post-Christendom: Church and Mission in a Strange New World* (Carlisle: Paternoster: 2004), p.314

72 1 Kings 19:12–18
73 Acts 10:9–20
74 Heart2Bless, see www.bless.org.uk
75 Revelation 22:2
76 Michael Frost and Alan Hirsch, *The Shaping of Things to Come* (Hendrickson Publishers, Inc., 2003)
77 Michael Frost and Alan Hirsch, *The Shaping of Things to Come* (Hendrickson Publishers, Inc., 2003)
78 Exodus 31:1–11
79 Ephesians 3:20
80 Dan and Dave Davidson and George Verwer, *God's Great Ambition* (Carlisle: Paternoster, 2002)
81 Rollie McKenna, *A portrait of Dylan* (London: J. M. Dent & Sons, 1982) p.68 ff.
82 *Chambers Twentieth Century Dictionary* (Edinburgh: W. & R. Chambers, 1972)
83 J. K. Rowling, *Harry Potter and the Philosopher's Stone* (London: Bloomsbury, 1997)
84 Tremper Longman III , *The NIV Application Commentary: Daniel* (Zondervan, 1999) p.167
85 NIV Expositors Bible Commentary, Zondervan, CD Rom
86 Alexander Solzhenitsyn, speech on receipt of the Templeton Prize
87 Walter Brueggemann, *Finally Comes the Poet: Daring Speech for Proclamation* (Fortress Press, 1989), p.117
88 Daniel 6:16
89 A term coined by banker Dee Hock, founder of the Visa network, to describe systems that combine elements both of order and of chaos
90 *Chambers Twentieth Century Dictionary* (Edinburgh: W. & R. Chambers, 1972)
91 Steve Rose, 'What a load of rubbish' in *The Guardian*, November 29, 2004, G2 p.13

[92] Roy McCloughry, *Living in the presence of the future* (Leicester: IVP, 2001)

[93] *Chambers Twentieth Century Dictionary* (Edinburgh: W. & R. Chambers), 1972

[94] Daniel 7:27

[95] Psalm 85:10

[96] *Chocolat*, A Lasse Hallstrom film

[97] Eugene Peterson, *The Message* (NavPress, 2004)

[98] Acts 1:6

[99] Acts 1:7,8

[100] Craig Bartholomew, 'Consuming God's Word: Biblical interpretation and consumerism', in *Christ and Consumerism: A critical analysis of the spirit of the age*, Craig Bartholomew and Thorsten Moritz Eds. (Carlisle: Paternoster, 2000), p.93

[101] Ephesians 3:10,11

[102] Ephesians 4:11–13

[103] Zechariah 8:13